PUBLICITY
for
nonprofits

GENERATING MEDIA EXPOSURE THAT LEADS TO AWARENESS, GROWTH, AND CONTRIBUTIONS

SANDRA L. BECKWITH

 KAPLAN) PUBLISHING

This publication is designed to provide accurate and authoritative information in regard to the subject matter covered. It is sold with the understanding that the publisher is not engaged in rendering legal, accounting, or other professional service. If legal advice or other expert assistance is required, the services of a competent professional should be sought.

President, Dearborn Publishing: Roy Lipner
Vice President and Publisher: Cynthia A. Zigmund
Acquisitions Editor: Karen Murphy
Director of Production: Daniel Frey
Production Editor: Karen Goodfriend
Interior Design: Lucy Jenkins
Typesetting: Elizabeth Pitts

Published by Kaplan Publishing

Printed in the United States of America

06 07 10 9 8 7 6 5 4 3 2 1

Library of Congress Cataloging-in-Publication Data

Beckwith, Sandra L.
   Publicity for nonprofits: generating media exposure that leads to awareness, growth, and contributions / Sandra L. Beckwith.
      p.   cm.
   Includes bibliographic references and index.
   ISBN-13: 978-1-4195-2299-4
   ISBN-10: 1-4195-2299-X
   1. Publicity—United States. 2. Fundraising—United States. 3. Endowments—Public relations—United States. 4. Nonprofit organizations—United States—Finance.   I. Title.
   HM1226.B427 2006
   659.2—dc22

                                                                    2005035736

Kaplan Publishing books are available at special quantity discounts to use for sales promotions, employee premiums, or educational purposes. Please call our Special Sales Department to order or for more information at 800-621-9621 ext. 4444, e-mail trade@dearborn.com, or write to Kaplan Publishing, 30 South Wacker Drive, Suite 2500, Chicago, IL 60606-7481.

PRAISE FOR *PUBLICITY FOR NONPROFITS*

"Packed with useful background information, compelling examples, insider tips, and easy-to-implement tools for publicity planning and implementation, Publicity for Nonprofits is a friendly guide for nonprofit managers."
VICKI WEISFELD, PRINCIPAL, NEW ASSOCIATES, LLC
FORMER SENIOR COMMUNICATIONS OFFICER,
THE ROBERT WOOD JOHNSON FOUNDATION, PRINCETON, NJ.

DEDICATION

To my daughters, Jessie and Alex Assimon

Contents

PART THREE

TACTICS

PART FOUR

THE PLAN

I'd like to thank the public relations practitioners and nonprofit organization leaders who so generously provided case studies and publicity tool samples for this book. I hope their work inspires others. They include:

Debbie Anglin
Jan Beckwith
Norman Birnbach
Judi Burns
Layne Cameron
Christopher Cutter
Todd Dezen
Ray Dorman
Abby Dress
Bill Goodwill
Victoria Hopta
Shel Horowitz
Justin Kazmark
John Kramer
Julie Ludwig
Michael Mahle
Andrea Pass
Brette Peyton
Elizabeth Philpott
Dave Platter
Jim Redmond
Amy Riemer
Howard Schiffer
Michael Smith
Randi Tucker
Barry Wanger
Jennefer Witter

Good publicity is essential to the success of any organization, but is especially crucial for nonprofits. Publicity can generate the kind of media exposure that leads to donations, grants, volunteers, and the best board of directors imaginable. It can mean the difference between an organization that thrives and one that just gets by. It can educate constituents and lead to reform. Good publicity grows from a well-thought out strategic plan that takes into account the organization's mission and goals and works to support them by communicating the right kind of information through the media at the right time.

This book contains everything you need to know to get the kind of publicity that will help your organization move forward. It's written for the types of individuals working at nonprofit organizations who have attended my "how-to-do-it" publicity workshops or called me for advice about some of the basic elements of a solid publicity program. These are the people in the "trenches"—those of you who not only have to come up with a publicity strategy and plan, but have to implement it, too. Many of you don't have a background in communications, yet,have to be master communicators.

It is light on theory and jargon and heavy on instruction. And because there's a lot of emphasis in the book on how to do it (not just why you should do it), you'll see that you can either read it from beginning to end, or go directly to the sections that strike a chord with your business goals today.

Use this book as your resource for the tools, tactics, and knowledge you need to get and keep your name, issue, or messages front and center. As you begin to take action with what you've learned, send me a note if you have questions. I'm happy to answer them. Contact me at sb@sand rabeckwith.com.

GETTING STARTED

1

WHAT DO YOU WANT
TO ACCOMPLISH?

What is publicity, and where does it fit into the marketing mix? Publicity is the subset of a larger category known as public relations. *Public relations* includes employee relations, investor relations, corporate communications, community relations, and other situations where an organization communicates with its publics. *Publicity* refers to free media exposure—those situations when your organization or cause appears in the news and editorial content of publications or on TV and radio news and talk shows.

Publicity differs from other communications options such as advertising and direct mail in that you don't—and can't—pay for it. You also can't control it. While some consider that lack of control a negative, most agree that the benefits of free media exposure far outweigh the risks resulting from the lack of control. Because of the implied editorial endorsement, some estimates put the impact of this media exposure at ten times the value of advertising because it offers so much more credibility.

Advertising, on the other hand, is time or space that you buy and control. You know what your advertisement or commercial will look like and say because you created it, and you know when it will appear. You have the same control over direct mail campaigns, too, because you write, design, and create the materials and decide when they are mailed and to whom. While these marketing efforts are worthwhile and have a place in a nonprofit's marketing plan, none has the impact of free media exposure—publicity.

None is as affordable as publicity, either. Costs associated with the simplest publicity plan might be a small chunk of a smart staffer's time. Elaborate fundraising events might cost more to publicize and should probably be supported with advertising and direct mail, too. But the constant with publicity is that you never have to pay to share your message on a radio talk show, you never have to pay for that compelling editorial about your cause that appears in the newspaper op-ed section, and you never have to pay for that 15-second sound bite on the 6:00 PM TV newscast.

Let's be realistic, though. That 15-second TV sound bite might have been pulled from a 5-minute interview. How do you make sure that the news department uses the 15 seconds you want them to use? And how do you make sure you deliver your message so clearly and compellingly that reporters seek out your perspective on issues your organization supports or fights? These are among the instances when this book will be invaluable to you and your organization.

IT'S ABOUT CONTROL

Publicity success is all about everything you do behind the scenes to control and shape the messages you present to the media outlets you hope will support your cause, your goals, and your initiatives. It's about what you can do to control your media outreach so you worry less about whether you got your point across in the interview and more about how you will share the resulting publicity with your board of directors without clapping with glee. It's about knowing what to say when you're caught off guard by a reporter and knowing how to say it when you're in the middle of a controversy. It's about putting a face on your story so that the media joins with you instead of working against you.

It's not hard to do. But it does take a thoughtful approach coupled with clear communication and practice, practice, practice. Most of us are so busy with our jobs that we don't have time to be thoughtful or strategic about our work, let alone create a work plan. We've got too much to do—too many items on our to-do list—to sit down and think, "Where does this activity fit into the organization's strategic plan, and what's the wisest way to reach our goals?" We want to check off those items on the list and move on to the next crisis, because there always *is* a next crisis. But as a wise philosopher once said, "Failing to plan is planning to fail." It works that way with publicity, too. Planning your publicity efforts is essential. The planning process makes certain that you're using your time as effectively as possible. It helps you see which tactics will bring you closer to your goals and which might look good to management but aren't really appropriate for your situation.

It's certainly tempting just to scan the table of contents and skip ahead to the chapter on news releases, because you know that most good publicity efforts rely on news releases to a certain extent, or to the section on how to write an op-ed, because you've got a great idea burning a hole in your head. But the wiser option is to stay here and read this chapter first. This is where you will ask and answer the questions that will give your publicity plan the focus it needs and where you will begin to discover which tactics will and won't help you reach your target audience and your goals. This is where you begin to get organized, both in terms of what you want to accomplish and how you will make that happen. This is where you do the up-front work that helps you create the visibility that leads to greater financial stability.

PUBLICITY PLAN ELEMENTS

This chapter addresses your organization's situation/overview, target audiences, strategies, goals, objectives, tactics, timeline, and budget. Read it with paper and pencil in hand so you can jot down answers as we ask questions—or as you think of questions. This approach will save you time later.

Situation/Overview

Begin the planning process by summarizing your organization's communications situation in one or two short paragraphs. What is happening with the organization that makes publicity a priority? Are you launching a new initiative? Have you determined that the community doesn't understand the cause you represent? Are you hoping to increase awareness of your group to pave the way for an upcoming fundraising campaign? Do you need the power of the press behind you as you advocate for change?

This is not the place to recall the organization's history, to regurgitate your mission statement, or to describe what the agency does on a daily basis. This is the place to say: "This is what's going on here. This is why we need publicity."

Target Audiences

Next, list your target audiences. These are your stakeholders. They might include the general public or people of a certain demographic or income level, current donors, potential donors, individuals who benefit from your services, local employers, your own employees, the board of directors, and so on. Prioritize your list of audiences, starting with the most important and working your way down.

Then consider which media outlets your stockholders read, watch, or listen to, because these are the media categories you'll be targeting. If your target audience is local teenagers, high school newspapers and the radio stations teens listen to will be more important to your plan than a regional lifestyle magazine or a National Public Radio affiliate. A national organization targeting women of childbearing age will want to include women's magazines or perhaps national television talk shows.

Strategy

What, exactly, is your strategy to garner publicity for your organization? Your publicity strategy will reflect your big-picture thinking and set the stage for your selection of tactics. Your strategy will summarize the direction you're going in one or two sentences. It might be to involve members of the local media in as many of your programs as possible. Or it could be to develop good relationships with the two or three reporters you think will help your organization the most in the long run. It could be to leverage the information resources offered by your national parent organization to generate local media exposure. Or your strategy might be to take advantage of the way dramatic television shows are increasingly including themes or messages related to your cause. You might want to create a communications committee that will be responsible for guiding or implementing your publicity efforts. Your strategy is overarching thinking that sets you on the right path.

Local Tigers Create International News

After a pet tiger escaped and was shot by authorities near a school in suburban New Jersey, its owner fought a losing battle to keep her remaining tigers. The International Fund for Animal Welfare (IFAW) was brought in by New Jersey authorities to move the 24 animals to a sanctuary in Texas.

IFAW leaders saw an ideal platform both for drawing attention to the problem of private ownership of big cats in the United States and for communicating its message about protecting wild animals. Using a strategy that turned a regional story into a national event and framed the story as symptomatic of a national issue rather than as a curious news item, IFAW generated hefty media coverage of the move. More than 1,500 stories ran worldwide with media impressions totaling more than 100 million. Most important, the publicity helped secure passage of the previously stalled Captive Wildlife Safety Act eight days after the New Jersey tiger move.

Goals

You won't know where you're going or what you want to achieve without setting some goals. A goal is a broad statement of direction that is determined by your needs. With good goals in place, you can look at each publicity tactic and ask, "Does this step help me achieve my goals?" If the answer isn't yes, the tactic should be removed from the plan. Goals are well defined but not specific or measurable. They tell you which direction to go, while your subsequent objectives will tell you how to get there.

What do you want to accomplish with publicity? Answer this question in bullet points. Sample publicity program goals might include the following:

- To use the local media to better educate consumers about this disease's warning signs
- To raise our profile so that we are in a better position to recruit top community leaders as board members
- To help generate ticket sales for the upcoming fundraising dinner featuring a celebrity speaker

With goals in place, you're ready to define the tactics that will help you reach those goals.

Objectives

Objectives are measurable targets set within a specific time frame. Objectives grow from goals to help determine your progress. Put in different terms, goals tell you where you want to go; objectives tell you how you're going to get there—and when. Publicity objectives must be stated in very specific terms to be meaningful and useful. They should outline the following in bulleted format:

- The expected accomplishment
- Who will do the work to make sure you succeed
- When the accomplishment will be finished
- How you will know the accomplishment has been achieved

To establish your plan's objectives, review your goals and then ask, "How will I make this happen?" If your goal is the first one listed above, "To use the local media to educate consumers better about this disease's warning signs," then sample objectives for this goal might include the following:

- By November 15, I will have placed one newspaper item or article and done two radio talk show interviews about the warning signs.

- By November 30, I will have secured a local TV personality with a personal connection to this disease to be the guest speaker at our fundraising luncheon.

Measurable statements allow you to monitor the progress of your activities as you work to achieve your goals. Adding deadlines helps you prioritize this work with your other responsibilities.

Tactics

Tactics are the "meat and potatoes" of your plan. Tactics are the *things* you'll do or the *tools* you'll use to get publicity. They're telephone pitching, press releases, tip sheets, op-eds, press conferences, newsworthy surveys, and so on. Tactics are the tangibles that will help you achieve your goals.

To select the right tactics, go back to your goals and objectives and ask yourself, "What do I need to do to make this happen?" If your goal is to advocate for change, consider a mix of tactics that includes controversial town meetings, op-eds, public affairs talk show ideas, a content-rich Web site, editorial board meetings, position papers, and public speaking. Review your tactical options and select those that meet your needs and your budget. Start now by listing tactics you're already aware of that will help you reach your goals. (If you're not aware of any, you'll learn a lot from this book.) Add to this to-do list as you read through the book. Subsequent chapters will help you learn more about what works best in which situations.

Budget

What is your organization's publicity budget? Do you have a realistic amount of money to spend? If no money has been set aside for this important effort, can you take money from other efforts and allocate it to publicity? It's important to know from the beginning how much money you have to spend, because this amount will determine how many and which tactics you'll use and whether you'll be able to hire a consultant.

The beauty of publicity, though, is that many of the tactics with the greatest potential impact require more time than money. That brings up an important question, though: if you don't have the money to pay for help, do you have the right talent in-house? You'll need a good communicator—somebody who writes well and isn't afraid to sell a reporter on an idea. Think in terms of volunteer resources, too—members of the board of directors, a volunteer communications committee, and so on. Some communities also have organizations that link marketing communication volunteers with nonprofit groups looking for help with specific projects. Some tactics, though, will require a budget, no matter who is on staff or how many experienced volunteers help out.

If your tactics are primarily time intensive, calculate how much time they will take so you can be certain you have the internal resources to execute them. If your final wish list of tactics exceeds the staff hours available, look again for volunteer help from the community. Your local chapter of the Public Relations Society of America should be able to help you find a volunteer (find your local contact at http://www.prsa.org). Does a local college have a communications program? Colleges are great resources for interns, but even if you need help with just one project for a few weeks or a month, it shouldn't be hard to find a student who wants to help in exchange for the resume-building experience.

Timeline

A time line will help you manage the tasks and tactics included in your plan. If you want your op-ed to appear during a certain week to coincide with a local or national event, for example, then note both your start date and your targeted publication date on your timeline. If you plan to mail one news release a month, let your timeline reflect not only the release schedule but when you need to start writing each piece.

Use a format that works best for your work style and personality. Some people like to use a month-by-month calendar; some like the long, stretching across-the-page historical timeline model; and others like to list the start date, the due date, the task, and the person responsible on a Word or Excel grid. Use whichever system will make certain that you execute the elements on time for maximum impact.

IT TAKES TIME

Publicity can be a real asset to your organization. But it won't happen overnight. Publicity that gets the results you want and need takes time, planning, effort, and follow-up. You might generate positive media exposure in just a few days, or you might need weeks or months. Your results will depend on some things you *can* control—the quality of the materials you use to communicate your news and information or the news value of your story—and others you *can't* control. These might include a train accident that diverts news crews from your press conference, an editor with a personal aversion to your topic, or SPAM blockers that won't let your e-mails through but don't send back a "no delivery allowed" message. Realizing that success doesn't come overnight will help you manage your expectations and those of your administration and board of directors. As you formulate your goals, objectives, and tactics, remember to factor in a realistic time frame for your results.

As you read on, you'll learn a great deal about the tools, tactics, and techniques needed to get the attention of the media. The rest of this book reveals how to create and use all three and which tools work best for which situations. Once you've learned more about them, you'll be in a great position to complete your publicity plan. We'll do that near the end of the book.

NEXT STEPS

Before moving on to the next chapter about what is newsworthy, take time to do the following:

- Write down the first half of your plan—the situation/overview, target audiences, strategies, and goals.
- Refer to this information as you read through the book.
- As you learn more, make any revisions to these elements.

2

WHAT'S YOUR NEWS?

A basic tenet of publicity is that your information has to be newsworthy. No news equals no media exposure. In addition, while your goal is to send the press information that is truly newsworthy, it's up to the media gatekeepers to determine what *they* think is newsworthy. Even if you think your organization has a story worthy of the front page, if the front page editor doesn't agree with you, it won't happen.

The trick is to learn how to think like the media—the editors, reporters, and producers you'll be contacting. It's not hard, but it does take a little effort. Begin by taking one example you consider newsworthy and ask yourself, "Who cares about it?" You care, right? That's one. But who else cares? Give it the neighbor test: if your neighbors saw your news in the newspaper, would they care? Is it interesting to the general population or just to employees of your organization? Would it be interesting to several people at your health club or just to the constituents served by your agency? Would the woman eating lunch at the next table find it interesting, or does it appeal only to your board members? For something to be newsworthy, it must have broad appeal.

STUDY YOUR TARGETED MEDIA OUTLETS

Next, spend some time studying the media outlets that are important to you. They might be local, national, or online. Again, it takes a little effort to do this, but it's relatively easy to fit your media studies into your daily schedule.

Watch the morning news programs on the local television network affiliates while you're getting dressed to see whether they do in-studio interviews between 6:00 and 7:00 AM or if they send reporters into the field for lighter feature reports. Read the local newspaper cover to cover while having breakfast to get a sense of what the editors and reporters think is worth covering. Listen to the radio talk shows you'd like to be interviewed on while driving to get a feel for the types of guests they like on their shows. Watch the early evening local TV news broadcasts every night for two weeks so you understand how the programs are structured and where your news might fit into the lineup. Notice whether any of them include a "good news" segment at the end of the half hour, because your story might be perfect for that. Monitor the Web sites or e-newsletters you'd like to cover your news so you're clear on what they use and don't use.

Studying your target media outlets serves another purpose as well: it will make you a better "pitcher" when you start contacting these outlets. If you've got something newsworthy to offer, you're more likely to see it in the news if you know how it fits into your outlets' formats. Media representatives are always more receptive to pitches from people who are familiar with their product than they are from those who are not. And, even if what you're offering isn't newsworthy enough, a reporter is more likely to explain why it won't work to someone who's obviously familiar with the media outlet.

Perhaps the easiest way to see what the press considers newsworthy from nonprofits is to start a clip file where you accumulate every news item you see that references any nonprofit organization, large or small, local or national. Do this only with your targeted media outlets. Clip from print publications and jot down notes from broadcast outlets, being certain to include the outlet, a few words on the news item, the time of day it ran, and whether it was part of a news program or talk show—and which one. You'll start to see a pattern emerging. Even better, you'll start to see how your organization fits that pattern already.

Caps for Caring

When Eric Pass was just 13, he created a volunteer project, Caps for Caring, in anticipation of his bar mitzvah. His goal was to collect 1,800 baseball caps to give to children battling cancer. Eric's mother, Andrea, supported his letter-writing campaign targeting sports teams and corporations by sending e-mail messages about the project to community news editors and religion writers at local newspapers. Reporters jumped on the touching human interest story. Andrea then expanded her reach by e-mailing notes to e-newsletters covering volunteerism, and Eric's story appeared in many of them. Because Eric is an associate member of Hadassah, the Women's Zionist Organization of America—which also accepts men as members—Andrea contacted that organization. It in turn connected her to editors of its many publications, which carried stories about Eric's campaign. In the end, the letter-writing initiative and the grassroots media exposure yielded more than 4,300 baseball caps to donate to a number of charities, including Hadassah Hospital in Israel.

Keep in mind that there are also varying degrees of newsworthiness. What is newsworthy for a newspaper won't necessarily appeal to a magazine or to radio or television news. Newspapers, because they're published daily or weekly, focus on very timely information (with the exception of feature articles in the living section). Monthly magazines, on the other hand, have a three- to four-month lead time, so they can't use breaking news. TV is a visual medium, so potential TV news items need to lend themselves to visual illustration. Only the most newsworthy stories make it to most radio news broadcasts (with the exception of all-talk stations) because radio stations use their very limited amount of news time to focus on hardcore news stories. They're lucky if they can fit in the latest shooting, layoffs, arguments between the mayor and the city council, and the accident on the interstate. Radio talk shows and public affairs programs offer more opportunities than news broadcasts for nonprofit publicity.

Table 2.1 outlines the types of news opportunities that are typically available to most local nonprofits and indicates which news outlets are most likely—or not—to be interested. These are only generalities, not certainties. For example, what is appropriate for an e-newsletter or e-zine depends on the publication's topic and distribution list, so one news item might work while another wouldn't. As far as national nonprofits go, some national magazines would certainly be interested in their news while they wouldn't care about the same news from a local nonprofit.

After you've become familiar with your target media outlets, you will have a much better sense of what's newsworthy. Newsworthy information offers reporters something timely, new, fresh, interesting, useful, amusing, instructional, entertaining, or moving. It's information that shows that what you're doing at your organization is unique, unusual, first of its kind, part of a national or local trend, or groundbreaking, or demonstrates that you have expertise that nobody else has. It's information that keeps the community up-to-date on topics they want to be informed on—health risks, safety threats, quality of life, and so on. The list of interesting topics goes on and on. Your challenge is to communicate your news and information on these topics in a way that makes certain it gets heard. (You'll learn more about how to do this in subsequent chapters.)

When generating ideas, keep in mind that bad news is more newsworthy to the press than good news. Think of how we become "rubber-neckers" when we pass a bad accident on the highway. We don't want to look, but we can't seem to stop ourselves from doing so. For some reason, bad news catches the world's attention more than good news. Yet most organizations want to keep their bad news to themselves—which is quite wise. You can take advantage of the popularity of bad news by wrapping your good news in some of the bad. If the good news is that there are fewer homeless people in your county, then start with the bad news first—there are still too many homeless people. If the good news is that your theater company raised the most money ever this year, package it in the bad news: you still need even more money to present quality productions. It might seem negative and even counterintuitive, but the fact is, you get more attention by emphasizing the negatives than focusing on the positives.

IDENTIFYING WHAT'S NEWSWORTHY

Let's start with what *isn't* newsworthy. As noted in Table 2.1, it depends on the media outlet you're targeting. In general, though, it's the

TABLE 2.1 *News Opportunities by Media Outlet Type*

News Item	Newspaper	Local Magazine	National Magazine	Radio News	Radio Talk Show/Public Affairs Program	TV News	TV Talk Show/Public Affairs Program	E-newsletter/E-zine
New hire or staff promotion	✓	✓						
Major grant announcement	✓	✓			✓	✓	✓	✓
Fundraising campaign launch	✓				✓	✓	✓	
Announcement of this year's board of directors	✓	✓						
Announcement of fundraising dinner with national celebrity keynote speaker	✓	✓*		✓	✓	✓	✓	✓
Tip sheet on how to do something better, smarter, faster, easier	✓	✓	✓		✓		✓	✓
Executive director comments on local implication of breaking national news story	✓			✓	✓	✓	✓	
Announcement of local participatory event designed to call attention to issue or cause	✓	✓*			✓		✓	
Announcement that executive director has joined government task force or other local committee	✓							

more routine, day-to-day things that might be exciting to a few within your organization or those it serves but don't have much relevance to the community at large; e.g., two staffers will attend a national conference, you've increased the number of parking spaces at your building, or the development director was named employee of the month.

So, what *is* newsworthy? Organizations often face two challenges when it comes to identifying what they're doing that might be newsworthy. The first is that management thinks everything is newsworthy and deserves a news release—or, worse, a press conference. (In fact, you should drop everything right now and send out a release announcing that your organization has just updated the text on its Web site.) The other challenge is that plenty is going on that could give your group media attention—but nobody's telling you about it. When you're not getting the information you need to give your nonprofit the media exposure it deserves, it's most often because the people with the information don't know it has news value or because the organization lacks a system for sharing news and information on a regular basis. You can do something about both problems.

If colleagues aren't aware that they're sitting on newsworthy information, you can help educate them by showing them your clip file. It's an easy way for them to see that what they're working on now is just as newsworthy as what is already in that file. They will also discover how much media attention other nonprofit organizations are getting, and this information could light a fire under the more competitive people in your group. Take your information gathering beyond their job description, too, by exploring what they do outside of work that might be newsworthy. Is the head of human resources competing in a national karate tournament? Does a case manager have a unique, interesting, or dangerous hobby—like extreme mountain climbing or collecting 1950s lunch boxes—that might lead to a feature in the newspaper's living section?

In addition, enlist the support of top management to establish a better communication system, because all new processes work best if they're endorsed by the people at the top. With that support in place, choose the information-gathering system that works best for you. This could be weekly staff meetings where colleagues share what's going on with their department or their projects. It might mean sending a biweekly memo to department heads asking what's new, interesting, surprising, or unexpected. Maybe you want to be copied on certain reports.

Make a plan based on your needs and the size of your nonprofit. Then stick with it, because if you don't know what's happening within the organization, you'll lose touch with any newsworthy developments and the opportunity to leverage them for exposure.

Sometimes, though, even when all of this is in place—and you're looking under rocks for news, too—you still don't have much going on to share with the press. There's not much you can do to keep your name in the news, right? Wrong. This is when it's actually *more* fun to get your name in the news—because it requires more thought and creativity. You're also more likely to be successful, because more creative newsworthy ideas can truly be more useful to the press than your regular news items. Here are some ways you can create your own news.

Write and Distribute a Tip Sheet

A tip sheet is a form of a news release that offers tips or advice in a bulleted or numbered format. This communications vehicle allows your organization to share specialized knowledge about an important topic with the public. It can be used "as is" by the print media, or it might be the springboard for an in-person interview with broadcast media. It's a way of sharing your expertise, which helps build credibility, goodwill, and trust.

You'll learn how to write and format a tip sheet in Chapter 6, but now's the time to think about the topics on which your organization can offer advice. Start a list—it's possible you could create one tip sheet a month in addition to your other publicity activities. When brainstorming for newsworthy tip sheet topics, think in terms of the brain trust in your organization. What do you advise people about—what's your expertise? What does your group do better than any other group? What are some examples of the advice you offer to constituents? If you work with the physically disabled, perhaps you advise businesses on how to make their facilities more accessible. Turn that advice into a tip sheet. If you run an animal rescue mission and teach volunteers how to recognize abused animals you can turn that knowledge into a tip sheet, too. Gather a few colleagues and bounce ideas off each other to get going. Here are a few more ideas to get you thinking:

- Museum: "The Five Best Ways to Experience Fine Art"
- Hospital: "How to Select a Doctor"

- Cancer care: "Six Things You Can Do to Decrease Your Cancer Risk"
- School: "Seven Things Parents Can Do to Help Children Become Better Students"
- Religious organization: "Five Reasons Why Doing Good Is Good for You"
- Local office of national disease organization: "Six Signs of [Your Group's] Disease and What to Do about Them"

Comment on National Headline News

One of the easiest ways to create news for your organization is to tap into existing national headlines by offering a local, expert perspective when the opportunity presents itself. Local media outlets are always looking for the local angle on a national story. If you're alert to how you can provide it, there's a good chance you'll get an interview. This kind of opportunity requires the ability to act quickly, though, so if your organization usually moves at a snail's pace, attempting to do this might create frustration. But for those who can respond to the opportunities as they appear, this tactic is an excellent way to build awareness of the organization and credibility for its leaders.

The tsunami in Southeast Asia at the end of 2004 is a great example of how media outlets appreciate the local news angle in a global story. Every hometown TV station and newspaper scrambled to find local residents with families living in the affected region or who had loved ones vacationing there. They also sought the expertise of local relief agencies for comments on what the world might expect in terms of global assistance and, most important, how local residents could aid the relief efforts. Local agencies had the opportunity to assist in a highly visible way. Other types of breaking news situations include study results released by medical publications such as the *Journal of the American Medical Association,* the *New England Journal of Medicine,* or one of the many specialty medical publications, or by research firms or think tanks.

If a group releases study results showing that TV remote controls emit damaging ions and your organization exists to advance men's health, you should jump on the chance to provide a local angle to your local media outlets. When a national group announces that fourth graders don't know the difference between George Washington and

Abraham Lincoln and your cause is youth literacy, use this announcement as your media soapbox. Watch a national TV news program every morning or scan an online news Web site to be on top of the day's headlines and see if there's an opportunity for your organization to be in front of a news camera today.

Tap into TV Storylines

How many times have you seen your issue or cause addressed as part of a storyline on a television show? It happens all the time for some groups. Today's television dramas, soap operas, and sitcoms reflect many of the real issues in today's world—the issues your organization is addressing. One of the best long-term examples of this is NBC's *ER,* a program with a remarkable impact on America's health knowledge. In fact, at one point, *ER* reported that two-thirds of the show's viewers watch it for health information and that more than half of its viewers say they have learned important health facts from watching the show. Knowing this, and knowing that the show's producers are careful to make certain that their medical information is accurate, many NBC affiliates schedule their health news updates for the newscast that follows *ER* on Thursday nights. A little sleuthing each week can help your nonprofit identify some of the health issues that might be addressed in one of the drama's three storylines each week and determine if there's potential for a news interview with the local perspective.

In recent years, the crime and law dramas have covered everything from animal rights to dementia to rape to obscure religions. *Scrubs,* a sitcom, managed to bring levity to advance care planning. *The West Wing* singled out Heifer International, a charitable organization that promotes sustainable development to end world hunger, and it addressed Oregon's assisted suicide law after it came under attack by then U.S. attorney general John Ashcroft.

As noted in many of their commercials, these shows really are "ripped from the headlines," and those headlines might be near and dear to your heart. Start thinking now about how to leverage their content to your advantage through news interviews, op-ed pieces, and community forums. You'll learn more in subsequent chapters about how to do this, but now's the time to start thinking about the publicity potential.

Do a Survey

Newsworthy survey results are sure-fire publicity starters. Big corporations know this. In August 2005, just in time for parents shopping for back-to-school supplies, Office Depot announced results of its survey on which celebrities parents would like to have tutor their children. This same survey could have been done by an organization promoting reading among children.

The key to success with these surveys is, once again, the word *newsworthy*. The results of a survey about how many of your church's members like Spaghetti-Os isn't newsworthy, but a survey on how often they attend church today compared with ten years ago has potential. The results of that survey can be used to pitch a story about trends in local church attendance and what they mean for your community. A survey of local moviegoers about the type of car they drive to the theater isn't newsworthy, but a survey about how they feel about violence on the big screen is both newsworthy and relevant for a group advocating less violence in entertainment. A group that links volunteers with people learning to read can survey volunteers or the community about the books they think everybody should read, providing inspiration and guidance for those just learning. A group that makes wigs from human hair for cancer patients could sponsor a survey about which celebrity hairstyle cancer patients want the most.

In addition to being newsworthy, the survey topic should relate to your organization's cause or mission. Environmental activists might survey supermarket shoppers about whether they prefer paper or plastic—and why. The survey results can generate news while providing the group with information it can use to shape communications messages based on people's perceptions or misperceptions. Think in terms of getting the most mileage from your efforts: what do you need to know from constituents or the community, and how can you make that information newsworthy?

State-by-**S**tate **R**eport **C**ard **M**akes **N**ews

The March of Dimes developed an annual state "report card" on new-born screening to generate media coverage on the topic, raise public awareness, and spotlight the nonprofit's advocacy efforts. To publicize report card findings, the organization developed a press kit, secured families having personal experience with newborn screening to do inter-views, and identified in-house spokespersons. The organization distrib-uted press kits nationwide to health/consumer editors and producers in both English- and Spanish-language markets. The media relations team supplemented this effort with e-mail pitches and phone calls to targeted media and with online chats and interviews. In 2004, the effort gener-ated coverage in *The Wall Street Journal,* NBC's *Today Show,* ABC's *World News Tonight,* the Associated Press and CBS radio networks, *Newsweek,* and *People.* Following the release of the report card in 2004 and again in 2005, the number of states providing more than 20 of the 29 March of Dimes–recommended tests rose from 9 to 23, helping to prevent death and disability in thousands of babies.

Create a List

Lists are popular with the media. David Letterman's "Top Ten List" gets reprinted the next day in newspapers coast-to-coast. When the Tor-onto Board of Trade wanted to weigh in on the provincial budget, it dis-tributed a widely used release titled, "Top Ten Things That Should Be in the Ontario Budget." This attention-getting, easy-to-absorb release let this credible source get its views heard. Lists can be serious or fun; they can show how to do it right or how to do it wrong. To communicate the need for clean water in a community, you can distribute a list of the top ways to *prevent* clean water, making certain that the list contains some of the procedures you'd like to change, or you can use a list of the top ways to make certain your community is *guaranteed* clean water, including methods not used that you'd like to see incorporated.

Take Advantage of Newsworthy Seasons and Holidays

Certain holiday stories run every year. For Easter, national TV news covers the Pope at the Vatican, and local TV news shows us an Easter egg hunt with cute kids. At Christmas, we see or read stories about coping with grief or loss during the holidays and learn all about great gifts under $20. Halloween brings us stories about the most popular costumes and how to keep our kids safe while trick-or-treating. It wouldn't be Memorial Day without a TV segment or food page story about the start of the summer grilling season or the Fourth of July without a warning about the dangers of fireworks. And in late August and early September, the media tell us how to get back to school. With the first snowfall comes instruction on safe winter driving. When the mercury climbs above 90, we learn how to avoid heatstroke. If it's spring, we're getting gardening tips or finding out how to get the yard ready for warmer weather. When it's fall, we're doing the opposite, preparing our homes' exteriors for the coming cold months.

Each predictable seasonal story brings publicity opportunities for nonprofits. A church with members planning to attend Easter Mass at the Vatican can facilitate a local newspaper article, a TV news interview, or a radio public affairs talk show interview on the trip. The local office of the National Center for Missing and Exploited Children can promote safe trick-or-treating practices. The Office on Aging can advise residents on how to look out for elderly neighbors during weather extremes. A group advocating for a more organic lifestyle can offer nontoxic alternatives to traditional lawn care in the spring and fall. The possibilities seem endless once you spend some time thinking about them.

Host a Contest or Competition

Contests and competitions offer multiple newsworthy publicity opportunities—you can get publicity when you announce the contest, when you conduct it (if it's an event), and when you proclaim the winner. The Special Olympics events are just one example of this—what media outlet doesn't want to provide exposure for this cause? But yours doesn't have to be a sporting event. It can be an essay contest for students, a search for the most heart-healthy recipe or ideas, your new nonprofit's name, a fishing derby that calls attention to the quality (or lack thereof) of local waterways—the list can go on and on. What will resonate with your stake-holders and the media at the same time? Come up with a fun idea and then get the most out of it.

NEXT STEPS

Before moving on to the next chapter to learn about message development, take the time to do the following:

- If you don't have a system in place to help you learn of newswor-thy events going on in your organization, take steps to set one up.
- Using the ideas in this chapter, make a list of at least five newswor-thy opportunities in your organization that could generate a cal-endar item or a large feature article.
- Schedule time with your most creative, imaginative colleagues to brainstorm more ideas.

3

WHAT DO YOU WANT TO SAY?

One of the essential early steps of publicity planning is message definition—figuring out exactly what you want to say through the media. What do you want to get across in your interviews or through your news releases? Your message could vary, depending on the situation and circumstances. In some situations, your goal might be to communicate a message related to your organization's mission or reputation. In other situations, your goal might be to communicate messages related only to a project or program you're promoting, not the entire organization. Regardless, here's the bottom line: if you aren't clear on your message each time you communicate with the media, your publicity efforts will be less effective. Careful attention to messages allows you to get a little more control over the unpredictable—and generally uncontrollable—publicity process. Anything you can do to exert some control is good.

If your organization is sophisticated enough to have a branding process or initiative, your overall organizational message will come from your brand positioning. Program messages will support that positioning but won't necessarily be the same as your organizational message. If you haven't gone down the branding path, your overall message is the one thing you want people to know about your organization, mission, or cause. What do you stand for? What do you want to be known for? What do you do better than your competition?

Keep in mind that your message—whether it's for the organization or a program or an initiative—has to be clear, simple, direct, and emotional. Too often, we get bogged down in the details surrounding the issue. We want to tell everybody everything we know about it, because it all seems so important to us. When it comes to message development, though, you want to remove all those details and focus on the heart of the issue. You want to zero in on the emotion behind the issue. You want to use language that will motivate an audience to take action instead of accepting the status quo. It doesn't matter if the language you use in your message doesn't motivate you or if it's language that is very different from your goal or mission. What counts is that it motivates your audience by striking a chord with them.

Another key point to consider is that, as noted in Chapter 2, bad news is more interesting to listeners than good news. People pay more attention to threatening news than to happy news. That means that a negative message gets their attention. You don't want to go too far, and you don't want to use this tactic when it's obviously inappropriate, but if you've got disturbing, attention-getting information that relates to your cause, don't be afraid to use it. If you're part of an environmental group working to keep a certain type of frog from becoming extinct and you're having trouble getting people to care about the slimy little bugger, perhaps you can craft a message that explains how once the frog is gone, another type of creature will probably disappear, too, and the chain will continue until one day, there will be no more housecats. Okay, that's a stretch . . . but you get the point. When you make your bad news relevant and personal, you'll be more successful than if you just say, "It's important that this frog not become extinct."

DEVELOPING YOUR MESSAGE

Message development can be as complicated—or as simple—as you want to make it. It's so important, though, that some organizations hire outside consultants to develop and test their communications messages to make sure they are meaningful and that they resonate with target audiences. If you don't have the resources for that type of support, you'll still be fine developing media messages on your own as long as you're methodical, thoughtful, and objective about it. Essentially six steps are involved:

1. Defining the issue
2. Creating draft messages
3. Testing the draft messages
4. Refining the messages
5. Testing the final messages
6. Adjusting the final messages

Defining the Issue

Defining the issue involves more than just stating your cause or position; e.g., "There are too many homeless people in our community." When developing your overarching message, you need to factor in what you do best for that cause. What is your SWOT analysis—your strengths, weaknesses, opportunities, and threats? This exercise serves two purposes. It helps you determine what you do best and where your nonprofit can find opportunities. It also helps you identify descriptive language for your organization, language that is very useful to the message definition process. What makes you stand out? What makes you different or better? Your message will play up your strengths, not your weaknesses, but you need to know your weak points, too.

Now look at your message from the perspective of your target audience. What do the people in your audience know about it already? What don't they know that's important? How do they feel about the cause? How does it affect them? What interests them about it? Don't assume you know the answers to these questions just because you've been involved with the organization or the issue for a long time. Interview a cross-section of your target audience, either one-on-one or in groups, to find out what they know and don't know and how they feel about the topic. This process will either validate your assumptions or open your eyes to views or perspectives of which you were unaware.

A large national foundation that was developing a communications campaign designed to educate the public about end-of-life care issues learned firsthand that research can redefine the issue. It hired a market research firm to meet with members of the initiative's target audience, women who were caregivers of individuals who were seriously or terminally ill, to assess their knowledge of the topic. Among other things, the market researchers learned that the women in the focus groups were unfamiliar with the term *palliative care,* a descriptor commonly used by health care professionals when referring to providing comfort when there's no hope for cure. Program leaders were surprised by this revelation—which in itself was a revelation. Leaders had forgotten that before they became involved with the issue, they had to look up *palliative care* in the dictionary, too.

It was an important development and one that assured two things. First, messages used in the campaign wouldn't include this piece of medical jargon. Second, the campaign would educate the public about the meaning of this key term, because the audience's health care providers did use it routinely.

Record your conversations with audience members to make sure you capture their own words as they respond. The phrases and language they use can be helpful as idea triggers when you're developing your messages. These recordings can also be valuable internally, when the information gathered runs counter to the organization's existing thinking. A colleague who disagrees with the conclusions of the research will find it harder to poke holes in a videotaped conversation than an interviewer's scribbled notes.

M*essages* M*ake* C*ampaign* E*minently* S*uccessful*

Eminent domain is the power of government to buy private property for a specified public use, such as the construction of a road or a public school. Increasingly, however, eminent domain is being used for private development instead. To call attention to eminent domain abuse, the Institute for Justice (IJ) worked through the mainstream media. Key to the campaign's success was consistent and constant use of IJ's messages. In all interviews, the organization's advocates delivered brief but compelling statements that offered both substance and analysis on an issue. Those messages included, "Eminent domain has gone too far," "Eminent domain is widespread," "The use of eminent domain for private development is unconstitutional," "We have to get back to a commonsense understanding that *public use* means something the public will own and use," and, "If this can happen to New London homeowners, this can happen to anyone. Will your home be next?"

In addition to researching target audience knowledge and impressions, gather as much statistical data as possible about your issue. Much of this might be available within your organization already. How many people in your community are affected by this problem? What percent of the total population is this number: 1 in 10 people or 1 in 100,000? If you are working with a local nonprofit corporation but can't get local statistics, get national numbers. Gather as many facts as you can to help you assess the impact of the issue on your audience. It is important to have facts, rather than anecdotes or gut feelings, when assessing the impact of the issue.

CREATING AND TESTING YOUR MESSAGES

Combine what you learn about your audience and its attitudes with what you know about your topic to brainstorm possible messages. Do this in a group, if possible, because people tend to become more and more creative when they're feeding off the ideas of others. Using the issue of too many homeless people in the community as an example again, you might have learned that your suburban audience turns its back on the homeless situation because individuals see it as an urban issue that doesn't affect them. At the same time, additional research on this subject might reveal that more families are closer to being homeless than they think. What if your research shows that 25 percent of all American families are just one paycheck away from being homeless? That would get the attention of somebody who felt it wasn't an issue that affected them, wouldn't it?

When brainstorming, think in terms of what action you want your audience members to take. Factor in what would motivate them to take those steps as well as their perceived obstacles to action. If you're seeking donations to a program that helps find jobs for homeless people so they can get off the street, and your audience's biggest barrier to donating is that the problem doesn't feel relevant to them, your message needs to show that it is. Here's a draft message for this: "Homelessness is a bigger problem than we imagined. Recent research shows that a full one-fourth of all American families are just a paycheck away from losing their homes."

If your goal is to get people to eat a more healthy diet, and your research shows that their biggest obstacle to doing this is their impression that healthy food takes more time to prepare and they don't have that time, your message has to address that obstacle. Here's a sample draft message: "Preparing a healthy meal doesn't take any more time than waiting in the drive-through line at your favorite fast food restaurant." (These hypothetical examples use made-up facts; make sure your messages are based on *real* facts.)

Creating Draft Messages

Create as many draft messages as you can. Capture all of them—don't discard any in the beginning. Once you've got a long list, review each very carefully. What seems vague? What resonates? Are there a few that everyone likes—and a few that everyone dislikes? Marcia Selva, founder of the Global Community Service Foundation, says that when she was defining the overall message for her organization, she struggled with a long list of options. She turned to a photographer friend for advice, asking how the photographer selected the best picture from the many good ones coming out of a photo shoot. The photographer said she puts all the possibilities on a wall and leaves them there. If anybody walks by and has the least bit of concern about one of them, it's discarded. She makes her selection from those remaining. Do the same thing—be thoughtful and critical of each possible message so that you winnow the list down to no more than a half dozen that everybody agrees might work.

Testing the Draft Messages

Test your short list with your target audience to determine what language resonates, which options fall flat, and which strike a positive chord. You can do this one-on-one in conversations or with a group. Present the messages to them one at a time and ask what they think of each. Ask these specific questions:

- What does this message mean to you?
- Does this message motivate you?
- Is there anything about it that confuses you?
- Would this message motivate you to take action?

As you did earlier when assessing your audience's knowledge of the issue, listen carefully for their questions, confusion, or affirmations. Take note of the language they use to describe things.

After reviewing each message individually with your test audience, present all of the draft messages collectively and ask them to select one they think does the job best. Ask these questions about the message selected:

- What do you like about that message?
- What don't you like about it?
- Is there anything missing?
- How would you phrase it differently?

The input from multiple sources—both internal and external—can sometimes be conflicting and confusing, but it's a necessary exercise. You want to be certain your message resonates with the people it's intended to motivate. The only way to do that is to make no assumptions and instead ask representatives of your audience what they think.

Refining the Messages

With the feedback from your message testing in hand, you'll know if you have one message that's dead-on, several that are popular, or a few that stand out and a few you can toss. Many times, you'll find that one or two rise to the top, and you'll have to decide which one to use. Sometimes, audience confusion or a misunderstanding with all of your test messages requires that they be redrafted. In still other situations, you've got at least one message that's almost perfect, but needs a little tweaking. Assess where you're at and make the necessary adjustments or changes—or move on happily with a message that has struck a chord with your group.

Testing the Final Messages

When you've selected a final message, test it with a larger sampling of people to make sure it communicates what you want it to. More sophisticated methods include random telephone sampling; but when you don't have the resources for that level of assistance, just reach out to more constituents than you did before. Ask them the same questions you asked when testing the draft message so you're certain that the final message communicates appropriately and doesn't confuse or mislead.

Adjusting the Final Messages

If there are problems when you test the final message, make adjustments and test again until it is right. When you've got it right, you're ready to weave the message into all of your communicational vehicles and efforts, including your publicity materials and media interviews.

Let this worksheet guide you as you develop your organization's messages. (A worksheet that can be photocopied is included in the Appendix.)

Message Development Worksheet

Message Point 1
Headline: _____

_____

Supporting anecdote, information, statistic, etc.: _____

Message Point 2
Headline: _____

_____

Supporting anecdote, information, statistic, etc.: _____

Message Point 3
Headline: _____

_____

Supporting anecdote, information, statistic, etc.: _____

USING YOUR MESSAGE WITH THE MEDIA

Now that you've put all this time and effort into developing and testing your message, you want to get your money's worth out of it by using it a lot, right? Good. That's exactly what you should do. Use it and use it and use it. Use it until you say it in your sleep. Then use it some more. A message needs to be repeated often to be remembered. You want your audience to hear and see it as often as possible. That means using it in all of the promotional materials involved with the program and using it in all of your media relations materials.

Keep in mind that this message is not a slogan or a campaign theme. It's information you want to share with your target audience to motivate them to take action, so when working with the press, use it in a conversational way. One way to do this is by quoting your organization's spokesperson in a news release. Going back to our earlier example of the organization that was trying to get people to eat more nutritious foods for health reasons: we can use that message in a news release as a direct quote from the executive director.

Let's say you work for the (fictitious) Healthy Foods Council of Summit County and the *Journal of the American Dietetic Association* has just published an article with shocking new statistics about the prevalence of obesity in American teenagers. Your organization can respond to these statistics by distributing a press release that summarizes and supports the *Journal*'s findings, and offers solutions to the problem. The release can quote your leader repeating your message in this way: "Preparing a healthy meal doesn't take any more time than waiting in the drive-through line at your favorite fast food restaurant,' said Martha Brown, (fictitious) executive director of the Healthy Foods Council of Summit County." The release can go on to offer advice or tips.

Messages can be woven into the language used in news releases or other press materials. The message above can be stated as a fact, rather than as a quote, in this way: "The Healthy Foods Council of Summit County reports that preparing a healthy meal doesn't take any more time than waiting in the drive-through line at a fast food restaurant."

Messages can also be used in pitch letters designed to generate articles on a subject. In this case, the message could be part of the opening statement in a letter sent to the health reporter at a daily newspaper, encouraging her to write a feature on local teen obesity—the causes, the cures. Here's how the letter might begin:

> In the August 6 issue of *Journal of the American Dietetic Association,* authors of an article titled "The Teen Obesity Epidemic" assert that teenagers need better nutrition and more exercise. The dieticians at the Healthy Foods Council of Summit County couldn't agree more. In fact, they tell us that preparing a healthy meal for teens doesn't take any more time than waiting in the drive-through line at a favorite fast food restaurant.

If your message is true to the core of your issue or program, you'll find that it's easy to weave it into everything you send to the media.

Always, always, *always* use and repeat your message in media interviews, too. When Martha Brown is interviewed for the local evening news about the *Journal* report and its relevance locally, she will use her message as the answer to several questions. Whether the query is "How can teens avoid the obesity trap?" or "What can parents do to help?" her answer will be the same: "Preparing a healthy meal doesn't take any more time than waiting in the drive-through line at your favorite fast food restaurant." She can offer more specific tips or advice after sharing her message. Even if a reporter asks, "How many local teens are considered obese?" Brown can present her message first, then offer the local statistics. It's particularly important to repeat the message with TV news interviews, because a five-minute interview often gets edited down to a sound bite of just a few seconds. If your sound bite is attention getting and meaningful and gets repeated enough, chances are good that it will make it to the air.

NEXT STEPS

Before moving on to the next chapter about media outlet categories and the types of news and information they use, take time to do the following:

- Learn what your audience does and doesn't know about your issue. Identify important information gaps and understand what will motivate them to take action.
- Combine what your research reveals about target audience knowledge with what you know about your organization and its issue.
- Develop and test draft messages.
- Refine your message and test again.
- Incorporate your messages into written materials and media interviews.

TOOLS

4

TO WHOM WILL
YOU SAY IT?

Publicity is all about reaching your target audience through the media. That's why it's so important to know what your audience reads, watches, and listens to. It's also important to know how the different types of outlets gather and report the news, so you understand when and how to approach them. Your publicity's success will depend on what outlet you're trying to reach and whether it uses the kind of news or information you'd like to share. Combining what you learn here with what you learn by studying the outlet's content will help you determine how you might need to massage or tweak your story so that it gets used and your message gets out there.

WHO USES WHAT?

It helps to have a good understanding of the different media types, typical demographics, the type of information they generally use, and whom to contact at each. (See Table 4.1 for an overview.) Use this information to compile a media distribution list or database in a format that allows you to add notes so that each subsequent pitch or submission is more effective. Remember to update your list regularly, too. In addition to making changes as you work with the list, call each outlet on your list every six months to confirm that you have the correct contact. There is always turnover that you might not be aware of. You want your list to be as current as possible.

Newspapers

Most communities have either a daily or weekly newspaper. These outlets are a good way to reach a large number of people because, according to Scarborough Research, more than half of Americans read a newspaper during the week and 62 percent read one on Sundays. Newspapers have strongest readership among people 65 and older and those with college degrees. They have the least penetration among people ages 18 to 34 and with Asians and Hispanics. To generate more readers in the younger and immigrant demographics, a handful of newspaper publishers have created special news products for younger people while others are now offering Spanish-language editions. In addition, some independent newspapers serve only Hispanics and only Asians. Many markets also offer alternative newspapers that appeal to younger readers.

Newspapers are news sponges, making them attractive targets for publicists. And because they reach half the population and have readership in most demographics—although that readership is lower in some groups than in others—they are usually a must for groups seeking media exposure. Newspapers also cover a wider variety of topics than most media outlets, so they are more likely to be interested in your story than, say, the local business magazine. Newspapers' division into content sections for national, local, lifestyle, sports, and business news illustrates the depth of subject areas covered by both daily and weekly newspapers. Newspaper interviews might be long or short, depending on whether the reporter is counting on you for background or just an opinion or pithy quote. But because newspaper interviews are often longer than TV interviews, you have more opportunities to repeat your message.

Send your news to the beat reporter who covers your topic area (education, religion, health, etc.) at the paper. If nobody is assigned to that topic, send your news to the section editor.

Magazines and Print Newsletters

Magazines are typically published monthly, bimonthly, or quarterly. Specialty print newsletters might be published weekly or biweekly. Because they focus on a particular subject or on a range of subjects for very specific audiences, and because they don't publish as frequently as newspapers, magazines and newsletters use less material. That's both good news and bad news. It's good in that what they want could be a perfect fit for what you're offering. In addition, the publication's audience might match yours perfectly. It's bad in that it will take at least three months to see your news or story in print. Also, you have to plan far in advance when dealing with these publications. If you're promoting your church's ethnic food festival in June, for example, you'll want to contact national magazines at least six months in advance and local magazines four or five months beforehand.

Who reads magazines? Who doesn't is more like it, according to the 2005 Spring Mediamark Research, Inc. Weighted Population (000) study. Women lead men, with 87 percent of women reporting they are magazine readers versus 81 percent of men. College graduates and people ages 18 to 24 tie for greatest level of readership, at 91 percent. Readership begins to drop slightly after age 24, down one percentage point each decade to age 64. It drops further, to 77 percent, for people 65 and older. Caucasians are at 86 percent, African-Americans are at slightly less at 83 percent, Asians at 81 percent, and Hispanics at 71 percent.

The type of information that magazines use from nonprofits varies from publication to publication. Local business magazines use announcements of new hires or promotion, but most other magazines don't. Most magazines run short news items in the front or back of each issue but only if the news is relevant to the majority of its readers and is not breaking news that will be useless by the time the issue is printed. All magazines contain articles with varying approaches or formats—informational, how-to, profile, question-and-answer, personal experience, service, and so on. Nonprofit organizations have many opportunities to use magazine articles to call attention to their area of expertise or their leadership. Magazine and newsletter interviews are similar to newspaper interviews—sometimes long, sometimes short, depending on the needs of the writer. Longer interviews provide more chances for you to repeat your message.

It's not always obvious who at a magazine should receive your information. If the publication has a small staff, send your material to the editor by name. When there's a larger staff, send article ideas to the articles editor by name. If you have appropriate news for the news section, find out who edits that section and send it to that person by name. (Sometimes the editor is listed on the section page, but sometimes you have to call and ask.) Print newsletters often have smaller staffs than magazines, so send to the newsletter's editor.

Radio

Radio is an important and powerful medium because it is so pervasive—there are nearly one billion radios in U.S. homes and cars, and Internet broadcasting has reached an expanded audience. In addition, radio often reaches people who lack access to other, more costly electronic mass media such as cable television or the Internet. According to the Radio Advertising Bureau, 94 percent of all consumers listen to radio every week. It is most popular with men ages 25 to 64 and women ages 25 to 54. Teens like it, too, with 71 percent of them tuning in daily.

Radio is an excellent vehicle for communications plans targeting upscale consumers, with 96 percent of adults with incomes greater than $50,000 and 96 percent of adults with college degrees listening weekly. Consider it, too, when targeting African-Americans or Hispanics with your message. Radio reaches 95 percent of African-Americans 12 and older each week; they spend an average of 23 hours per week listening to their favorite stations. Radio is especially strong with African-American women, reaching more than 97 percent in the 18 to 54 age range. The numbers are similar for Hispanic listeners; 96 percent of Hispanics 12 and older listen an average of 22.75 hours weekly, with more than 97 percent of Hispanic women 18 to 54 tuning in weekly. Radio is considered the gateway to the Latino community because of its penetration in this marketplace, where listeners appreciate Spanish language broadcasts.

Radio stations offer nonprofit organizations several ways to communicate their messages. Use longer format talk shows and public affairs programs to engage the public in conversation; promote an event, service, or product through a short, drive-time talk show interview; provide a local interview source for a significant breaking national or international news story; or submit a public service announcement (PSA) for broadcast.

For the most part, radio station news broadcasts will not be receptive to your pitches unless you're offering an interview with a qualified expert who can comment on big, breaking news or unless you're announcing a very, very large grant or donation. It's not that they don't care—they just don't have enough time, because the average radio newscast is just a few minutes long. Radio news interviews are very short, so reporters are looking for sharp, insightful comments. Talk show interview formats vary in length, from 3 to 60 minutes. Even though you have more time to express yourself in a longer-format talk show, you don't want to ramble. Listeners will lose interest. View a radio talk show interview as a conversation with a friend—keep it lively and interesting.

Contact the public affairs director for public affairs program ideas or PSAs, the talk show producer for suggestions for specific talk shows, the news director for breaking news interviews or big news announcements, or the show producer or host for short interviews during drive time.

Television News

The Pew Research Center for People and the Press reports that 57 percent of Americans watch local news broadcasts, 33 percent watch cable news, and 32 percent watch nightly network news. Like newspapers, television does better with older news hounds. People aged 65 and older are nearly twice as likely as those younger than 30 to have seen any news on television. Similarly, people of retirement age are nearly three times as likely as those younger than 30 to have watched the network evening news or morning news programs yesterday. With regards to local news, only 28 percent of viewers aged 18 to 29 watch it, while viewership is highest with those 65 and older. The next highest category is those aged 50 to 64, at 59 percent, and aged 30 to 49, at 41 percent. About one-third of all African-Americans and Hispanics watch the late local newscast.

While most local television exposure is short-lived, many local stations are extending the value of your interview by posting links to the Web sites of their news sources so viewers interested in more information can get it easily. This makes a brief TV news interview even more valuable. Your best possibilities for TV exposure include interviews on the morning newscasts that precede the network morning news programs (*The Today Show*, etc.) and noon news programs to promote an event or fundraiser. Evening news coverage works well for highly visual special events and spokesperson interviews related to hard news stories.

Public affairs program interviews also offer exposure. Some local broadcasts also set aside "good news" time to promote a local charity or nonprofit group at the end of a newscast.

Because TV is visual, you always have to think in terms of pictures when considering TV news possibilities. A "talking head" is acceptable when you're providing a local expert commenting on a breaking national story, but it won't work when you're hoping for coverage of your fundraising luncheon. Always think in terms of visuals that will help tell the story when you think you have something with TV news potential.

Bright **I**dea **R**eaches **M**illions

To create publicity for National Diabetes Awareness Month using broadcast outlets in New York City, the Juvenile Diabetes Research Foundation (JDRF) implemented a bright idea. It linked its knowledge of that city's television newscasts with an ambitious concept: lighting the top of the Empire State Building in blue and white—the JDRF's logo colors—in the middle of the designated month, November. The communications staff at JDRF knew that nearly every clear night, each TV weather forecast shows a live image of New York City during the broadcast. Most are shots of landmarks such as the Chrysler, Met Life, Citibank, Flatiron, or Empire State buildings. The blue and white lights offered a new visual that night, something the meteorologists, who have more time to ad-lib, could chat about. The idea worked. Meteorologists at all major New York City network affiliates covered the lighting and the fact that it represented National Diabetes Awareness Month. Understanding the needs of the meteorologists helped the JDRF reach nearly 3.5 million people with its message.

For news broadcast interviews, contact the assignment editor to suggest a timely news subject or interview. For in-person interviews during morning and noon news broadcasts, contact the show producer to suggest your idea. For public affairs program interviews and the "good news" segments, contact the public affairs director to offer your appropriate topic and spokesperson. Similar contacts apply to national network and cable TV talk shows and news programs. The morning network news programs also have segment producers who specialize by topic (health, lifestyle, etc.).

E-zines and E-newsletters

Electronic newsletters—e-zines or e-newsletters—differ from most print newsletters or magazines in that they are usually shorter, they often publish more frequently (many are weeklies), they have a much quicker turnaround time because they don't spend time at the printer, and they are highly specialized, making them appealing to publicists working to reach a narrowly defined audience. For example, there are e-newsletters for people who eat only raw foods, parents of children with diabetes, and crafters who want to sell their creations online. Find e-newsletters by starting at this Web listing: http://directory.google.com/ Top/News/Magazines_and_E-zines/E-zines/Directories/.

The quality of these publications varies, depending on the publisher. Some contain too much advertising or sales information to be useful, while others are the go-to source for any news or advice on the newsletter's subject. Most use announcements of events and new products, and many accept short articles. The best way to determine which ones you'll want to contribute to is by subscribing to several and studying each issue. This will also tell you what information would be appropriate for each. You are less likely to be interviewed by an e-zine editor and more likely to be invited to submit an article.

An e-zine or e-newsletter typically has a single editor to whom you'll send your news and information.

Web-based Publications

Many print publications and TV news programs have online versions, while many Web sites exist solely to provide useful content to specialized audiences. The online versions of print publications may contain some, none, or all of the print version's content, while some may contain additional and more timely news and information. Content-intensive Web sites, both local and national, are good targets for certain types of nonprofit news. A local arts council's Web site, for example, might maintain a calendar of events that will list your upcoming activity. A content-heavy national site, such as http://www.ldonline.org about learning disabilities, might use a short, relevant article bylined by the executive director of an appropriate, local nonprofit organization.

TABLE 4.1 *Media outlet overview*

Media outlet type	General demographics	Uses personnel announcements	Uses tips and advice	Uses general news releases	Does interviews	Person to contact
Daily newspaper	Broad reach but especially strong with older, college-educated people	✓	✓	✓	✓	Beat reporter or section editor
Weekly newspaper	Broad reach but especially strong with older, college-educated people	✓	✓	✓	✓	Reporter assigned to your community or the editor
Magazines	Very broad reach	Trade magazines do; consumer magazines don't	✓	✓	✓	Section editor or editor
Newsletters	Not available	✓	✓	✓	✓	Editor
Radio public affairs programming	Radio in general reaches most of the population		✓		✓	Public affairs director
Radio talk show	Radio in general reaches most of the population		✓		✓	Talk show producer or host
Radio news	Radio in general reaches most of the population			✓ (only big, breaking news stories)	✓	News director
TV news	Strongest with those 65 and older		✓	✓ (must have visual component)	✓	Assignment editor
TV talk show	Not available		✓		✓	Show producer
TV public affairs program	Not available		✓		✓	Public affairs director
Web-based publications	Varies depending on the site		✓		✓	Online editor

Some media Web sites offer contributors guidelines online that tell you how to submit an article. Some sites also list the name of the online editor, the person to contact. In most cases, however, you will need to contact the Webmaster or use a general inquiry form or address to find out who should receive your news, information, or article ideas. Web articles are shorter than their printed counterparts, so an interview is likely to be shorter than what you might experience with a newspaper or magazine.

COMPILING A MEDIA DISTRIBUTION LIST

The amount of time you spend developing your media distribution list and the resources you use depend on whether your list is local, regional, or national and whether you will be distributing your news by e-mail, fax, or regular mail. E-mail is the easiest, quickest, and least expensive way to distribute news, but some outlets still prefer to receive information through the mail.

The best way to compile a local media list is with a week's worth of daily newspapers, recent copies of weekly and alternative newspapers, local magazines, and your computer. Go through the newspapers and magazines to identify the reporter who covers your topic area. If it's not obvious, call the publication and ask for the newsroom or the editorial department—anyone who picks up the call can tell you who should receive your news releases and story ideas. Expand from there by either going online or pulling out your phone book. Online, you can often find a list of local media outlets by Googling the city, state, and the phrase *local media.* For example, Googling *Columbus Ohio "local media"* yields a site that lists all the media outlets with e-mail and Web site links for every city in Ohio. One site, http://www.us-npl.com/, allows you to select the state you're interested in to find most—but not all—of a state's media outlets. Most media Web sites offer either a general news room e-mail address or specific addresses for each reporter, so by clicking around a lot, you can compile a database with names, e-mail and snail mail addresses, and phone and fax numbers.

When you can't find an online listing for your city or when using the Internet isn't feasible, turn to the phone book. Look for sections labeled *Newspapers, Magazines, Radio Stations, and Television Stations.* Call the radio and television stations to get the name of the person you need and their e-mail address. After you've compiled your database, if the list is small enough, contact each individual by phone or fax to ask how they prefer to receive news releases—by e-mail, fax, or regular mail? Indicate that preference in your database and make sure you honor it. Update those preferences as you get feedback from those you weren't able to contact.

Larger media lists might require more resources. If, for example, you want to send your news to the education reporters at all U.S. daily newspapers with a circulation greater than 100,000 or to all the magazines targeting social workers, you'll need a media directory. These are expensive to acquire, but most libraries have at least one of them in the reference section. One of the best is the Bacon's directories (one each for magazines, newspapers, radio, and TV/cable). Others include *Burrelle's Media Directory, Gale Directory of Publications and Broadcast Media,* and *Gebbie Press All-In-One Media Directory.* John Kremer lists more options, including *Bradley's Guide to the Top National TV Talk & Interview Shows,* at http://www.bookmarket.com/directories.html. Bring a laptop and input the data on-site or photocopy the pages you need and bring them back to the office. When your list is long, either option is time consuming but not overly challenging, making it a good assignment for an intern or volunteer. Several companies, including Vocus, provide sophisticated software tools that let you create media lists, distribute your information, manage e-mail campaigns, track results, and evaluate outcomes. They are quite expensive and better suited for large-scale endeavors.

Firm Sculpts Media Outreach for New Museum

When businessman Raymond Nasher created the Nasher Sculpture Center in Dallas as a home for his impressive sculpture collection, the museum retained communications agency Richards/Gravelle to build interest and excitement for the opening. The firm used attitude research to conclude that it needed to make the topic more accessible while building buzz for the museum as a trendy destination. It developed a list of 2,000 media contacts prioritized in order of importance. Linked to that list was a master pitch calendar with story angles refined to each outlet's audience. In addition, the firm created a "who's who" community relations database of people to invite to grand opening events. The firm shared extensive press kits and key messages, initially with long-lead publications and later with more than 130 journalists attending a preview one week before the opening. This careful cultivation of a tiered list of media contacts supplied with an appropriate flow of information generated more than 500 print, online, newsletter, and broadcast stories surrounding the opening.

PRESS RELEASE DISTRIBUTION SERVICES

If you plan to do large mailings infrequently and don't need to maintain a mailing list in-house, it is usually more cost-efficient to use a press release distribution service. Which one you use depends on the media outlets you're targeting—radio and TV, daily newspapers, trade magazines in a certain industry, general interest publications, and so on. Knowing the categories for your media list will help you find the most appropriate or affordable option. Here are some popular options.

Bacon's (http://www.bacons.com/contact/distsrvbymail.htm, 800-621-0561). Bacon's e-mail news release distribution service is one of the most cost-effective for mass mailings. The cost to send an e-mailed news release is a minimum of $100. To put that in perspective, the cost to send a release to all U.S. daily newspapers with circulations greater than 50,000 is about $125. Bacon's will send you a media catalog that allows you to select the outlets for your distribution list. You can also send them a list of publications you want to contact and let them find the appropriate name and e-mail address in their database.

PRNewswire (http://prntoolkit.prnewswire.com/publicaffairs/). PR Newswire is a members-only service that waives the usual membership fee for nonprofits signing up through its Public Affairs Toolkit option. Membership includes multiple listings in ProfNet's Expert Database, a service that links reporters with story interview sources, a useful resource for any organization seeking a national presence. It also includes a complimentary target list distribution with the purchase of the nonprofit's first news release distribution using one of the larger domestic mailing lists. Release distribution costs vary; the standard news release that runs about 400 words can be sent to all media in your state; trade publications; and more than 3,600 Web sites, online services, and databases for as little as $150. If targeting a national audience, you can send to thousands of media points across the country for around $625. While national distribution includes additional services such as search engine optimization, all releases receive additional services such as reports on the number of times a news release is accessed by the media on PR Newswire's Web site.

Business Wire (http://www.businesswire.com). Costs to use this service depend on the size of the distribution list and the length of the announcement. The minimum charge is $160 for distribution for any metropolitan region other than New York City or northern or southern California.

PRWeb (http://www.prweb.com). This service suggests that users pay what they think the service is worth. Certain services, including distribution through PRNewswire (see above), are based on predetermined fees. If you don't pay at least $30, though, your release does not get sent out to the media. Instead, it resides on the Web site where media people could come across it. You want the release to be sent out, so plan on spending at least $30 and consider spending more, depending on the level of service you need.

Send2Press (http://www.send2press.com/PRservices/pricing. shtml). The distribution service offered by Send2Press that is most comparable to the example provided in the Bacon's description (daily newspapers) includes other media outlets but costs more—$149. Its lowest rate—$69, highlighted on the home page—is for releases sent within a state and is therefore most useful for regional news.

Majon (http://www.majon.com). Like other electronic distribution services, this one is best used for large-scale, national release distribution, which begins at $249. A statewide distribution option costs $199.

XPress Press (http://www.expresspress.com). Use this electronic distribution service when you're distributing nationally. $225 gets your release sent to 800 to 4,000 reporters.

MEDIA RELATIONSHIPS

Publicists are namedroppers. They love to talk about who they know in the media, because they believe it gives them a certain cache—and it certainly does in some circles. They are wise enough to tell potential clients about their media connections, because most people believe that

it's not *what* you know, it's *who* you know. But that's only half the story
when it comes to media relations. What's most important to know on
the topic of media relationships is that, yes, if somebody knows and likes
you, that person will be more receptive to your calls and pitches. However, if what you're pitching isn't newsworthy, you aren't any more likely
to get your story in the news than a total stranger who calls cold with a
great story. Having media friends is great, but having media friends *and*
a newsworthy story is what gets your organization the media exposure
it deserves.

You've already learned about what's newsworthy and what isn't,
and you're working to make sure you're consistently identifying news
opportunities in your organization. Now how do you establish relationships with reporters, editors, and producers who are important to you?
First, begin by identifying the media contacts that are most key to your
publicity objectives. If you've got a media list of 15 to 25 outlets—a
good range for a medium-sized city—determine which 3 or 4 are most
crucial to your success. They could be the daily newspaper, the
monthly magazine put out by the local archdiocese, the National Public Radio affiliate, and the TV station that is strongest with people
older than 40. Or it could be the alternative weekly paper, a chain of
weeklies, and the two radio stations that are most popular with teenagers. If you have a national audience, it could be a national association's magazine, a specific e-newsletter, and a trade publication.
Here's how to start connecting.

Introduce yourself. Begin the relationship-building process by
calling the contacts and introducing yourself. Keep it brief—just say who
you are and that you'll be sending information of value from time to
time. Encourage the contacts to call you with questions about anything
related to your organization or field; promise you'll send them an e-mail
with your contact information that they can save. Your only mission with
this call is to let contacts know that they can find a responsive contact
person at your organization.

Be a trustworthy resource. Make sure you send only information
that is relevant to that outlet. TV newscasts don't typically report on personnel changes at nonprofits unless you're announcing the new head of
the United Way, so don't send a press release about a personnel promo-

tion or new hire to any TV assignment editor. Make sure that you've completely fact-checked everything you send to the press so that your sources can count on you to provide accurate information. Double-check name spellings, event start times, and so on.

Help them do their jobs.   Just as you would for a friend who's interested in a particular subject, send your handful of key contacts news or information that they might be interested in but probably aren't aware of. You might pass along articles from trade magazines, links to news items on Web sites, or excerpts from an e-newsletter. It's important that this information be relevant to the reporter's job—you don't want to send material just for the sake of being in touch. But if you know that the reporter covers health issues regularly and you just learned that a nationally known health guru will be making a private presentation to employees of a local corporation, pass along that news.

Do as much of the work for the reporter as you can.   When you're pitching a story, include a list of other resources. These can be "real" people who will put a face on the story and who have already agreed to talk to a reporter, national associations, or other local experts who can provide informed commentary. This information makes it easier for the reporter to start the story and lets them see that you understand their job.

Return media calls promptly.   First, this is what friends do for each other, right? Second, if you don't respond, the reporter will move on to the next resource on the list and forget about you. Be accessible and, except in situations where it's not prudent to do an interview, be forthcoming. Share information.

Meet face-to-face once in a while.   Invite your media contact to lunch and use the time to learn more about that person's job, responsibilities, and interests. What stories is she working on now? What's her dream assignment? What's coming down the road? How can you help her? It doesn't have to be—and shouldn't be—all about work, but the more you know about her job, the more likely you can help her out, even when helping her doesn't get your organization media exposure. It's a "good karma" kind of thing. Besides, it's always good to know a little more about the personal interests of people when you're cultivating relationships. This is how business contacts lead to genuine friendships.

Say thank you. Everybody likes to hear those two words. After a newspaper has used your press release or a radio talk show host has interviewed you or a colleague, send a brief thank-you note. Media people receive so few of these that the ones they *do* receive stand out.

SHOULD YOU OFFER AN EXCLUSIVE?

There might be times when you consider giving a story exclusively to a particular reporter, whether because you know her media outlet reaches more people than any other, because that outlet's audience matches yours, or because you've developed a close relationship with the reporter. Sometimes in very competitive markets, one outlet will insist on an exclusive, saying that if you give it to anyone else, it won't run the story. This demand can be intimidating, especially if the outlet is the best fit with your target audience. But is it ever appropriate to give your news to one outlet exclusively? This question requires thought, because your decision could have long-term consequences.

When you give an exclusive, you're doing a favor for the reporter who gets the exclusive. At the same time, you might be alienating other media outlets in town. While the reporter who has the scoop looks great to the boss, those you've slighted are criticized by their bosses for not getting the story. In most cases, you have little to gain and much to lose by offering an exclusive. It is usually wiser to release the news to everyone at the same time and let them do with it what they will. As for the outlet that insists on exclusives only, if it's your most important outlet, consider offering an occasional exclusive on a story you know most of the other outlets won't be very interested in anyway. It's one way to keep a strong relationship while doing the least amount of damage.

NEXT STEPS

Before moving on to the next chapter explaining the various ways to package your news and information, take time to do the following:

- Determine which media outlets do the best job of reaching your target audience(s).
- Compile a media database in a format that allows you to add notes from conversations with your contacts.
- Identify a handful of contacts that are most important to your organization.
- Develop a strategy for developing and maintaining relationships with those contacts.

5

HOW WILL YOU SAY IT
IN MEDIA MATERIALS?

Organizations that use the standard publicity tools well have the most media success. While one tool is the telephone, used to pitch article ideas, most standard tools are written materials. News releases, tip sheets, pitch letters, press kits, and other tools all give media gatekeepers something to read and review, helping them determine if your material is newsworthy. It also helps them see what other information they need to gather to report the story accurately and objectively. This chapter describes and explains the different written communications tools you'll consider for your publicity plan. Because news releases and pitch letters are the most commonly used—and the most useful—they will be explained in greater detail in Chapters 6 and 7 respectively.

The process of figuring out what tool you need for which job will be easier if you use the guidelines outlined here and tune out Internet chatter about the worth of these various tools. While technology has had a profound impact on how we communicate with the media in the past several years, it hasn't altered the fact that we still need to use a journalistic writing style and materials that journalists recognize as news sources.

NEWS RELEASES ARE FOR NEWS

News releases, also known as press releases, are used to make news announcements. Perhaps you've hired a new executive director or have just received a significant grant from a national foundation. You'll share that news with the media through a news release that contains the relevant information—and nothing more. In printed form, a news release is typed double-spaced, giving a reporter room to edit or make notes, on your letterhead with a contact name, telephone number, and e-mail address in the upper right corner. Place a release date or the words *For Immediate Release* in the upper left corner, directly opposite the contact information. A catchy, attention-getting headline separates the contact information from the body of the release and entices the reporter to read on. News releases that are e-mailed should be single-spaced in the body of the e-mail message. Never e-mail a release as an attachment unless a reporter asks you to.

Because news releases are so commonly used, they are also quite commonly abused. To avoid having yours tossed in the recycling bin, follow the specific writing instructions in Chapter 6 carefully. Avoid the most common news release mistakes, including sending one that lacks news, putting the news at the end of the release instead of at the beginning, committing factual errors, and writing the news release as if it's an advertisement rather than a news story.

TIP SHEETS OFFER ADVICE

Tip sheets, a specific type of news release, are one of the most productive yet overlooked publicity tools. Because they are so useful, they are addressed in greater detail in Chapter 6, along with other kinds of news releases. A tip sheet offers advice or tips in a bulleted or numbered format. A nonprofit organization that works to keep children safe might send out a tip sheet on "Six ways to protect your children from the most common threats," while one that advocates for more informed patients might distribute "Five questions to ask when selecting a doctor." The information offered in tip sheets is often used in "news notes" columns of newspapers and magazines or as the genesis of a larger feature on the topic that incorporates the tips as well as an interview with the expert offering them.

News **R**elease **T**riggers **T**sunami **R**elief

Vitamin Angel Alliance, an organization that provides nutritional supplements to fight vitamin deficiency diseases around the world, including childhood blindness caused by vitamin A deficiency, launched a major publicity drive the day after the 2004 tsunami in Southeast Asia. The group committed to providing the nutritional component of the humanitarian relief effort. To do so, Vitamin Angels used PRWeb.com to send a news release soliciting children's vitamin donations. The release, sent to a nationwide media distribution list, was quickly picked up by nearly 900 media outlets, including industry magazines and key Web sites featuring nutrition industry news. Vitamin donations began arriving at the organization's warehouse within 24 hours. Five weeks later, Vitamin Angels had collected and began distributing 10 million supplements to tsunami survivors in Sri Lanka, India, and Indonesia. The group's quick use of a press release played a key role in lessening the likelihood of opportunistic infections and disease after the disaster.

Tip sheets are prepared the same way as a news release—double-spaced with contact information at the top of the page and a headline between the contact information and the body of the release.

PITCH LETTERS SELL IDEAS

A pitch letter is used to sell a reporter, editor, or producer on an article idea. As you'll see in Chapter 7, a pitch letter captures the journalist's attention in a page or less by being captivating and compelling. It tells the media gatekeeper about the idea, why it's important, and why the outlet's audience will be interested. A pitch letter must be long enough to summarize the idea but not so long that it overwhelms the reader with information. Pitch letters are often accompanied by additional background information that helps a reporter decide whether or not to pursue the idea. That additional material might be a news release, a press kit, or news clipping on the overall subject or interview source.

FACT SHEETS GET TO THE POINT

A fact sheet is either a list of bulleted facts that takes the place of a news release, or a list that expands on a topic covered in a pitch letter or a news release. The latter is supplemental information that saves reporters from having to find the facts on their own. Either way, it's essential that fact sheets contain just that—*facts*. A fact sheet should never include opinion or advertising hype.

Fact sheets are often e-mailed or faxed to a reporter as part of a story pitch—perhaps you call the reporter with a story idea, then follow up with the facts in bulleted form. This approach is favored because, quite frankly, it's easier to drop the facts into bulleted points than to write a coherent news release. In certain situations—for example, when you've sold the reporter on the story idea—it's also more effective than a news release.

Facts sheets are also included in press kits and placed on Web sites for online information seekers. A press kit announcing the formation of a nonprofit organization might include a fact sheet that lists important details such as the name of the executive director and other key staffers, the address, the mission statement, funding sources, initial programs or projects, and media contacts. An organization sending a pitch letter to a local newspaper proposing an article about the importance of good pain management and how to get it might include a fact sheet with national pain statistics—how many people report suffering from pain, how many do nothing about it, how many doctors are trained pain specialists, the impact of pain on the economy through lost work hours, and so on.

Use a fact sheet as supplemental information when you want to make a case for your idea or when you need to share a great deal of factual detail.

BACKGROUNDERS AREN'T NEWSY

Backgrounders contain just that—background information that is useful but not necessarily newsworthy. Because backgrounders are not designed or written to contain news, they use a different format from that of a news release. A backgrounder has a descriptive heading such as "Backgrounder: About the Organization" or "Backgrounder: Speaker Bios." It is typed double-spaced. A backgrounder might provide short narrative biographies of the speakers at a conference or the leaders of an organization. It might tell the history of an organization or campaign. It might explain an initiative's funding sources. Regardless of the topic, the backgrounder is written in a narrative form to provide additional information in an enlightening way. It is usually included in a press kit or attached with a pitch letter to provide additional information. Backgrounders should be included in the "media" section of an organization's Web site as well.

USE PRESS KITS WHEN A RELEASE ISN'T ENOUGH

Use a press kit when you're announcing news and there's too much information for a single news release. A press kit always contains at least one news release and at least one other element—a fact sheet, backgrounder, photo, tip sheet, another news release, news clippings, and so on. Virtual press kits are simply electronic Word documents that are e-mailed or posted on the organization's Web site. Hard copy press kits consist of an inexpensive two-pocket folder holding the various elements. By adding a label to the front with your logo and the subject of the press kit, you'll have a useful handout at a press conference or editorial board meeting.

Press kits are also useful when asking reporters to consider your spokesperson for media interviews. A spokesperson press kit should contain a cover letter summarizing your spokesperson's credentials and what topics that person could be interviewed on, a short narrative bio, a photo of the spokesperson, and a backgrounder on the nonprofit organization. A hard copy lets the reporter add your information to a paper file; but offer to provide the documents in electronic format for those using an electronic filing system.

Be careful to include only the information that's relevant to your announcement. Novices often tuck every brochure the organization has into the folder pockets. This is a waste of your materials, because reporters throw them away. Reporters don't use brochures for information unless there's nothing else to work from. If your brochures contain useful information that you want to share with the press, retype the text into a backgrounder to make sure it gets noticed.

Some publicists provide their press kit materials electronically as PDF files readable with Adobe software. Using Word for Windows is a better option, because Word files are easier to work with than PDF files. Copying, cutting, and pasting from a PDF file is harder, and anything you do to create work for a reporter takes you farther away from achieving your publicity goals. Regardless of the file format, always ask before sending press kit attachments. A better option when distributing electronically is to paste the text of all elements into an e-mail message or provide a link to the elements in the online press room on your Web site.

MEDIA ALERTS ANNOUNCE EVENTS

While the term *media alert* has become synonymous with *news release*, a media alert is actually a memo-style announcement that alerts the press to an event and its details. By using a different format than a news release, a media alert lets you flag the essentials for the media so they see quickly why—and where and when—they should send a reporter, photographer, or TV camera to an event. It can be used as an event invitation or as follow-up to an invitation. It is particularly useful as a reminder a day or two before the event.

Use a "who, what, when, where, why, and how" format to communicate specifics in a single-spaced format on letterhead. Start with "Who:" in boldfaced letters followed by a short answer to that question. Below that, state "What:" and describe what will happen at the event. Explain each of those five *W*s and one *H* in a way that, for example, lets a TV news assignment editor see at a glance that your event will be highly visual and interesting to viewers. Will newsworthy people be available for interviews? Include that information, too. At the end, tell the press whom to contact now for more information and whom to contact on site at the event for interviews or other information.

Because media alerts are more timely than news releases, you should fax them to newsrooms.

OP-EDS EXPRESS OPINIONS

Op-eds—opinion pieces that appear on the "opinion and editorial" pages of newspapers and in some magazines—are popular communication tools for nonprofit organizations. They are first-person essays that express an opinion on a timely issue or topic. Op-ed section editors look for well-written essays with strong and varying opinions on topics that will resonate with readers. They particularly like essays on controversial topics that people are talking about today.

An op-ed is an appropriate communication tool for your organization when you want to influence public opinion and policy or encourage change. Begin the essay development process by determining your topic, because there might be many your organization could address. An agency that advocates for the elderly, for example, might discuss the need for more affordable housing as easily as it tackles the problem of elder abuse.

With your topic in mind, determine your goal. What do you want to achieve through a published essay? What is your desired outcome? Do you want people to vote a certain way? Do you want them to behave differently? Do you want them to take a specific action? Next, plan how you're going to get to your goal through the written word. A good starting point is your message. Select one message, and only one message, to communicate. Op eds are short—typically 500 to 800 words—so you don't have room for more than one message. (While 800 words might seem long at first, once you start putting your passion to the paper, you'll wish for more space.)

With your topic and message in place, call an op-ed section editor to ask if she would consider an essay on your topic. This step will save you from writing about a topic the paper isn't interested in. Note that, while editors generally don't want yet another essay on a topic that has been well covered already, they are usually open to a fresh perspective or view. If you have something to say that hasn't been said before, make that clear. This conversation, in addition to saving both of you time and frustration, also gives the editor an opportunity to offer tips on what works and doesn't work for that publication.

Once you get a green light—even a tentative green light—take time to read back issues of the publication you're targeting for the style, tone, and structure of its essays. Your op-ed piece is more likely to be accepted if it's similar in format to those that have already been published.

Next, do an outline. Keep in mind that your essay should tell readers how the situation helps or hurts them. Imagine you are speaking to neighbors who are unfamiliar with the subject. What is the most important point your neighbor needs to know about this issue? Why should this matter to them? What facts or statistics might shock them? What action do you want them to take? While there are no hard and fast rules to follow about how to write an op-ed, here's a format you can use as a guideline:

- *Begin by illustrating how the topic or issue affects readers.* One good way to do this is by putting a face on the issue. Whenever possible, start the essay with the story of somebody who has been affected. If you're trying to get a traffic light installed at a busy intersection, start with the story of an individual who was seriously injured in an accident at that spot. If your goal is to help people understand the value of a single-sex education, begin with an example of somebody who floundered at a co-ed school, then began thriving at a single-sex institution. When putting a face on the story isn't appropriate or possible, lead with an attention-getting statement that shows how the topic affects readers. Make sure it's not boring or ho-hum—you want to capture readers' interest.
- *Follow that illustration with a statement explaining the broader scope of the issue.* Use statistics to put the situation in context. For that traffic light essay, your statistic might be the number of accidents at that intersection in a five-year period compared to an intersection with comparable traffic flow that has a traffic light. The single-sex education essay would benefit from statistics that illustrate how test scores improve when students change to a single-sex school or how classroom participation increases.
- *Describe the problem and why it exists.* This is often where you can address the opposing viewpoint—"There's no traffic signal because the highway department says it's not in the budget"—and your viewpoint—"but with the lives of our children at stake, we can't afford to accept that answer."
- *Offer your solution to the problem.* Explain why it's the best option.
- *Conclude on a strong note.* Repeat your message or state a call to action.
- *Add one or two sentences that describe your credentials as they relate to the topic.* Examples: "Marcus Brown founded Citizens for Traffic Signals after his wife was seriously injured in an accident at the Route 22 and Smith Road intersection," or, "Jennifer Jones is principal of the Madison Academy for Girls."

Editors like essays that don't need a lot of editing. Make certain yours is acceptable—and has the impact you want it to have—by avoiding language that is more academic than what appears in a daily or weekly newspaper. Avoid buzzwords and industry terms. Keep those neighbors in mind while you write so that your word choices make your message accessible to all readers.

Submit your op-ed electronically via e-mail whenever possible but always when your topic is very timely. If your essay is appropriate for more than one publication, you may submit to several as long as the publications don't compete for the same readers. Multiple submissions are most appropriate when your organization serves a multicounty area with many daily or weekly newspapers whose circulations don't overlap. If your op-ed is very timely, follow up by phone or e-mail in a day or two if you don't get a response. For those that are less timely, wait a week before following up. If your essay is rejected, ask for constructive feedback so that your next submission is more appropriate.

PUBLIC SERVICE ANNOUNCEMENTS (PSAs) ARE FREE ADVERTISING

Nonprofit organizations "own" public service announcements— PSAs. The PSA is defined by the Federal Communications Commission as "any announcement . . . for which no charge is made and which promotes programs, activities, or services of federal, state, or local governments . . . or the programs, activities, or services of nonprofit organizations . . . and other announcements regarded as serving community interests." These media announcements can be used to call attention to a social issue or to alert listeners to events such as a fundraiser or a town meeting. They can be "evergreen"—usable any time—or time sensitive because they're linked to an event. The longest-running PSA features Smokey Bear, who began telling us in 1947 that, "Only *you* can prevent forest fires." Decades later, in response to a rash of wildfires caused by careless campers, the last word in the PSA slogan was changed. The new message is, "Only *you* can prevent wildfires."

PSAs run free of charge on radio and TV and in print publications as a public service of those media outlets. PSAs must be noncontroversial, from an organization that is respected, of interest to a large and diverse audience, and in good taste. PSAs on anything controversial— topics such as abortion, gun control, and assisted suicide come to mind— won't be used because they might alienate an outlet's audience.

Print PSAs look like ads and are produced the same way you would create any other kind of advertisement. The most popular sizes are smaller; offer them camera-ready in horizontal and vertical formats so the publications have more options. For radio and TV, supply them as both script and audio. For TV, supply them on videotape in 60-, 30-, 20-, or 15-second lengths. Variety in length gives the stations more flexibility.

Many stations will help you produce your PSAs if you provide a script. You can also work with a local advertising agency, which might donate its services. This type of pro bono work serves the ad agency too. It helps build morale among employees who appreciate the opportunity to make a difference, it's good for community relations, and it's an excellent way for the firm to showcase its creativity to your board members and others. If you're paying an agency to create your PSAs, make sure it has experience with this type of communications vehicle, because PSAs differ greatly from traditional advertising.

Ad School Student's PSA Broadens Awareness

A pro bono PSA campaign created by an advertising student at Ad2 Miami, a subdivision of the Greater Miami Advertising Federation that provides education, networking, and leadership opportunities to students and young advertising and marketing professionals, helped the Miami-based Non-Violence Project USA, Inc. (NVP) spread its message to new audiences. NVP teaches alternatives to negative behavior by motivating and engaging youth in high-need, high-crime areas. This effort makes their community safer and healthier. The five 30-second PSAs in the "Hello Campaign" were designed to raise awareness of NVP with Miami-Dade County public schools, police departments, and social service agencies. They illustrated the reality faced by most at-risk youth—that without intervention, the majority will perpetuate the same mistakes made by their role models. Airing nationally and later used with 5,000 local students as part of a mentoring program, the PSAs successfully encouraged other nonprofit, social service, and community-based organizations to mentor and support children and adolescents living in high-need, high-crime jurisdictions throughout Miami-Dade County.

If you're creating your organization's PSA yourself, use simple, conversational language (contractions are good). Read your script out loud to make sure it avoids awkward language and too-long sentences. Type each script double-spaced on the right side of the page, with a separate page for each length. Put a heading at the top with the script title and its length. Include information on when you want it to air, with a start and end date, particularly when the PSA is promoting an event. PSA formatting doesn't use paragraphs and/or indentations, so leave them out. Make sure you include the pronunciation for names that aren't obvious. If it's hard for you to visualize what this should look like, ask the public affairs director at one of your radio stations to send one from the files so you can duplicate that format.

For broadcast PSAs, send your script or tape to the public affairs director by name, not title. At print outlets, send it to the advertising director. Package your PSAs so that they are noticed and remembered when they arrive at the outlet by including a cover letter that explains the issue being addressed and why running the PSA will benefit the community. When submitting to TV stations, include a storyboard so the PSA can be viewed without watching the tape. After your PSA runs, be certain to send a thank-you note.

Learn more about PSAs at http://www.psaresearch.com, a content-rich Web site maintained by a public service advertising consulting firm.

COLUMNS EDUCATE AND INFORM

A column is a short article that runs regularly in a newspaper or magazine. It can express an opinion—as those of syndicated columnists do—but it doesn't have to. It is usually written by the same person or covers a single topic each time it runs. Columns are written to educate and inform, but because they are open to opinions, they can also be used to influence others. Columns are expected to be based on the personal experience or professional knowledge of their writers, so they can include the writer's advice in a way that a reported article can't. A regular column in a daily or weekly newspaper is an appropriate communications vehicle for a nonprofit with a large audience and a mission that affects many. An elected official, for example, might write a weekly column for a community newspaper about what's happening in the town's government, while the head of the local humane society might address a wide range of pet topics.

Some publications, including local weekly business magazines, provide opportunities for one-time columns, but in most cases, a column is ongoing. A regular column is great exposure for both the writer and the organization; however, it requires not only good writing skills but a long-term commitment of time and column ideas. Don't propose a column to your local newspaper or a target Web site unless you know you can generate an almost endless supply of topics and you have the time to write the column on a regular basis, whether that's weekly or monthly.

To secure a column, put together a package of material that includes a compelling pitch letter, a short narrative biography highlighting your expertise, a list of 12 to 15 representative column titles, and your first three columns (these are essential—you need to show you can do the job). E-mail (no attachments) or mail this information to the section editor if you're targeting a daily newspaper or the editor of a weekly newspaper, magazine, or Web site. Call or send an e-mail two weeks later to follow up.

Write your column around the message you want to communicate for that column's topic. If you're writing the humane society column during Halloween week, for example, an obvious topic is how to keep your pets safe from the nastiest trick-or-treaters. Your message might be that, "Pets don't enjoy Halloween nearly as much as humans." Build your article around that message by outlining your thoughts, then writing an interest-generating lead paragraph (first paragraph) followed by your best advice. Wrap it all up with a conclusion that ties back to the lead. Column length depends on the publication, but most are no longer than 650 words.

Show your sample columns to someone you think is a good communicator and ask for constructive feedback. You want to present the best product possible when selling the idea to a publication and when you submit each regular column in the future. Sometimes, all that's needed to go from just okay writing to really good writing is input from an objective friend or colleague.

BYLINED ARTICLES GO IN-DEPTH

When it comes to publicity, there are two kinds of articles—those you write, and those that are written by someone else. Both types are valuable to any organization seeking media exposure. There are two big differences between the two—other than the byline. First, when you write the article yourself, you control the content. You can't do that when someone else is the writer. Second, fewer markets exist for articles written by people who are "experts" and not professional writers, which limits your possible outlets. Expert bylined articles are usually options in trade magazines; newsletters (both print and electronic); Web sites; and a small number of newsstand or consumer magazines. Most consumer magazine content is generated by professional writers (exceptions are usually experts who use ghostwriters or who happen to be good writers, too), and nearly all daily newspaper content is written by staff writers.

To be interviewed by a staff or freelance writer, you have to pitch the appropriate editor at the publication on a story idea that is appropriate for that outlet. Begin by studying several issues of your targeted publication carefully so you know what it does and doesn't cover as well as the types of articles it uses. Next, determine what you (or your organization) know that would benefit the readers of this magazine or newspaper but hasn't been covered already by that publication. Use the table of contents of past issues to help you shape this into a storyline or two or three. Present the idea to the right editor through a pitch letter. (See Chapter 7 for specifics on using and writing pitch letters.)

And who is the right editor? Editor names are listed on the publication's masthead. Sometimes it's obvious whom to send your idea to, but other times it's not. If it's not clear, call the main number and ask, "I'd like to submit an article idea. Whom should I send it to?" Get a name and e-mail address. Follow the instructions in Chapter 7 and send along your letter and supporting material.

The process for placing a bylined article is very similar. The only difference is that, instead of proposing in your pitch letter that you (or your colleague) be interviewed for the article as an expert source, you're proposing that you write the article based on your knowledge and additional research. Your pitch letter, then, will need to include one or two sentences explaining why you're the most qualified person to write the article. If your pitch letter flows logically and is coherent, this won't be a hard sell to a publication that is used to working with experts who aren't also professional writers. They expect to edit and polish the submissions of topic experts.

Once your idea is accepted, it's time to roll up your sleeves and start writing. Begin by writing an outline that matches what you proposed in your letter—the editor doesn't want any content surprises. Determine what information you need that you don't have and do the research to get it. Organize your notes and research according to the outline, then start writing. Make certain that your first paragraph is interesting and enticing so that people read on. If you're not certain how to begin, pull out those back issues of the magazine and study how other writers began their articles. One of those approaches will certainly work for you.

Include transitions between paragraphs so your text flows smoothly and with logic. Write to the specified word length—you will probably hit it before you know it—and give your article a strong conclusion. While some writers like to end with a strong summary quotation from an interview, others like to tie the conclusion back to the first paragraph. Look at those back issues again to see how your editor likes to end articles and follow that approach with yours.

Submit your article electronically by the specified deadline. Attachments are usually okay when submitting a completed article.

NEXT STEPS

Before moving on to the next chapter to learn how to create compelling news releases and tip sheets, take time to do the following:

- Become more familiar with the various tools described on this page. Go to the Appendix to see samples, and ask media friends for samples from their mail.
- Begin thinking about which tools will fit with your plan goals and budget.
- Start a list of ideas you might turn into news releases, op-eds, and so on.

6

HOW WILL YOU SAY IT IN A NEWS RELEASE

The news release is the most commonly used publicity tool. The acknowledged standard for communicating news and information to the media, it's a tool you'll want to use because it's instantly recognizable in any newsroom as a document that *might* contain something readers, listeners, and viewers want or need to know about.

Experienced publicists talk about the utilitarian nature of news releases—they are useful in so many information-sharing situations. Yet you'll find chatter here and there about the death of news releases. The thinking is that they are outdated tools that aren't necessary now that any individual—or organization—can post thoughts online in a blog (more on blogs in Chapter 10), reaching an audience directly instead of through media gatekeepers. They have a point. Blogging makes sense in certain situations—when you're communicating with an audience that spends a lot of time online, for example. But even then, you still need news releases to communicate facts and news to journalists. And while some journalists say they hate news releases, most will say that a good one still helps them do their job. Your job, then, is to learn how to write good news releases.

News **R**eleases **H**elp **S**ave a **M**ountain

When a local developer announced a plan to build 40 large homes on ridgetop land abutting a state park, neighboring resident Shel Horowitz formed a not-for-profit organization, Save the Mountain, and used news releases and other communications tools to do just that. After announcing the new organization in a news release that was used by the local media and generated attendance at the group's first meeting, Horowitz sent out nearly 20 more promoting the group's various activities. During the 13-month campaign, the news release–based media relations effort to save the mountain generated almost 70 print articles and two dozen TV and radio news reports or interviews. This exposure was instrumental in helping to mobilize thousands of people and stop the development project. When a wealthy benefactor stepped forward to preserve the land by buying it from the state, she stated publicly that she was inspired by the group's efforts.

having to follow up to get essential information. In most cases, you should be able to say what you need to say in 500 words or less (about two pages double-spaced). Good news releases are used as is, without further input from the organization. Good news releases can also generate large articles, which require interviews and research, too. Your goal is to produce news releases that make a reporter's job easier. Not every news release you produce will be used, but once you've gotten the hang of it, you'll see that most of your information is used in one form or another.

This chapter explains essential news release elements, provides writing tips, and outlines the standard news release format. It also explains how to create an effective tip sheet, a type of news release that offers tips or advice in a bulleted or numbered format. While news releases offer news, tip sheets offer how-to information. Tip sheets are often overlooked by organizations without much publicity experience, but nonprofit publicity pros see tip sheets generating positive media exposure time after time.

A news release should contain a contact name, phone number, and e-mail address for more information; a great headline; an attention-getting lead; specific information; a quote; and a concluding boilerplate paragraph that describes your organization. Here's what you need to know for all of these elements.

START WITH THE NEWS, FOLLOW WITH FACTS

A news release by definition must announce something newsworthy. (See Chapter 2 for more on what's newsworthy.) If it doesn't, it will be deleted. When that happens, you've wasted your time—and time is something most of us don't have a lot of.

Start the news release writing process by being clear about what news you're announcing. We'll use a hypothetical situation as an example so you can see how this works. Let's say your publicity strategy includes showing potential funders that your organization is vital, viable, and worth funding. One way to do this is to announce when you receive grant money—sharing this news allows you to illustrate that you have passed muster with other donors. You'll want to share this news through other communications vehicles, too, such as your newsletter and your Web site, but you'll definitely want to reach a wider audience by using the local media. The news we're announcing, then, is that your organization, the Fonda Food Bank, has received a $20,000 grant from the Acme Foundation. We'll write it together using standard news release elements.

Contact Information

Start with the easy part—put your name, phone number, and e-mail address in the top right of the page/screen. Use one line for each. Most people remember to include this information on printed press releases but for some reason omit it when they place the news releases on the organization's Web site. This is frustrating for reporters, who want to use the information but have questions and don't know whom to call to get answers. Make sure this media contact information is included in the online version of your release. In addition, repeat it at the end of the news release if you're e-mailing it, so the reporter doesn't have to scroll back up to the top to find it.

On the opposite side of the page, in the upper left, type in all capital letters FOR IMMEDIATE RELEASE. In some situations, you will ask reporters to hold the news until a certain date or time. In those cases, you will type FOR RELEASE ON and then add the date.

Catchy Headlines Count

The headline comes next, about two inches below the contact information. A reporter or editor looks at the press release headline first, and if it doesn't grab their attention, they toss it into the recycling bin quicker than you can shout, "Wait! This is really interesting!" *Do* agonize over your headline. Show it to others and get their reaction. Does it make them want to read on? Does it pull them to your opening paragraph? Use active and colorful or energetic words. Make it exciting, but don't exaggerate.

Some release subjects don't lend themselves to exciting or dynamic headlines. The goal then is to make sure the headline says as little or as much as it needs to. For our announcement, an appropriate headline would be "Acme Foundation Grant Allows Fonda Food Bank to Expand." Notice the word *expand*. It's a good word to use because it suggests positive change and growth. Your "expansion" might not involve anything nearly as dramatic as the word suggests, but the truth is, any significant grant will allow for even the smallest amount of expansion in your organization. Notice, too, that we've included the name of the funder in the headline. It's a small but essential way to show appreciation for your funding source. You'll do that in the body of the release, too, but recognizing the donor upfront is a wise development move.

Bad headlines for this topic might be "Fonda Food Bank Announces Donation" or "Nonprofit Receives Dollars." Both of these are vague and flat. They don't indicate the significance of the donation—and if there's no significance, you shouldn't send a news release.

The Lead

Begin your first paragraph with something called a "dateline," which is basically just a reminder of where and when the news is coming from. The format is CITY (capitalized) and state abbreviation, followed by dashes, the date of the release, and more dashes. Here's ours:

FONDA, Wisc.—October 10, 2007—. The release text begins after that second dash.

Your lead—the first paragraph—is next. Craft an attention-getting lead without worrying about including all the details. Start with a general statement, then move into specifics. Work to get the five *W*s and one *H*—who, what, when, where, why, and how—into the first two paragraphs. Concentrate on writing simply, as if you're talking to a friend or relative. Our lead might be, "The Fonda Food Bank announced it has received a $20,000 grant from the Acme Foundation in Waukesha. The grant will be used to buy additional freezers for donated food being distributed to an increasing number of area families who don't have enough to eat."

When the subject lends itself to a clever lead, use one. For example, a nonprofit working to help unemployed workers change professions might be presenting a series of workshops on how to deal with change. The lead, "The only kind of change some people like is the kind that jingles in their pockets," is more interesting than, "Career Shifters announces five workshops on how to deal with change," although the latter is certainly accurate and acceptable.

Supporting Facts and Statistics

When possible and appropriate, use statistics and facts to support the premise of your news release. This adds to the newsworthiness of your announcement, can illustrate the seriousness of the problem, and puts the topic in context for a reporter. In our release, we want to help readers see that many people in our area are hungry. The more shocking the number, the better. So our next sentences are:

Demand for the Food Bank's services has increased 20 percent every year for the past 5 years as the number of homeless or unemployed area residents continues to climb. In 2006, local homeless shelters reported that they served 1,500 more people than the year before, while the county reported that unemployment was up 8 percent.

Include a Quote

A quote from a leader of your organization is often appropriate for news releases, especially those announcing large donations, research or survey results, and tips or advice. The quote can amplify information already presented or express an opinion, but it should add to the information already presented, not repeat it. News release quotes come to us in three ways. We can interview the executive, we can use one of our message points to create a quote, or we can create a quote in the executive's absence because we know what's important to say in this situation and have permission to say it for the leader. Always get approval on quotes from the person you're quoting so no surprises result from memory lapses or poor judgment.

We will quote two individuals for our release—our executive director and the head of the foundation providing the grant. Both are important for news and development reasons. First, we want to say how much we appreciate the gift. Second, we want the donor to explain why our organization is worthy of the donation. This requires interviewing the foundation leader, which can be done easily over the telephone. The next part of our release, then, reads:

> "We are pleased that this donation will help us continue our mission, which is to link our region's food bounty with those in the area who cannot provide for themselves," said Frank Schmidt, executive director of the Fonda Food Bank. Martha Redler, president of the Acme Foundation, added, "We have seen firsthand the contribution this organization makes to our community and are pleased to be in a position to help the Food Bank expand its reach to even more needy people."

Include Your Message

Be certain to include your message(s) in the release. In the text of our example release, it could have been in the lead paragraph—"an increasing number of area families who don't have enough to eat"—or in the Frank Schmidt quote—"We link our region's food bounty with those in the area who cannot provide for themselves." Don't let your release go out without making sure you've included that message somewhere in a way that makes sense.

Conclude with Organization Description

Always conclude your release with a descriptive "about us" paragraph that is devoid of hype or exaggeration. Include this paragraph at the end of every release. It should explain what your organization does and why and include information that helps you stand out from other nonprofit groups. Are you the first? The only? Such descriptors are important. Because our release announces a grant, we also want to include a descriptive paragraph about the funder. Here's what we've got:

Founded by Joseph J. Acme in 1948, the Acme Foundation is Fonda's oldest foundation. It provides funding for programs that help the poor and the elderly.

Our next paragraph reads:

The Fonda Food Bank provides food to those who need it most. This year, the Food Bank will solicit and distribute more than one million pounds of food to thousands of individuals through senior centers, after school programs, and soup kitchens.

At the very end of the release, include one of two recognized graphic representations for the words *the end*. Use either three pound sign symbols separated by one space each (# # #) or a hyphen, the number 30, and a hyphen (-30-). Center this on the page.

Finished Product

Here's what the body of our finished news release looks like:

Acme Foundation Grant Allows Fonda Food Bank to Expand

FONDA, Wisc.—October 10, 2007—The Fonda Food Bank announced it has received a $20,000 grant from the Acme Foundation in Waukesha. The grant will be used to buy additional freezers for donated food being distributed to an increasing number of area families who don't have enough to eat.

Demand for the Food Bank's services has increased 20 percent every year for the past 5 years as the number of homeless or unemployed area residents continues to climb. In 2006, local homeless shelters reported they served 1,500 more people than the year before, while the county reported that unemployment was up 8 percent.

"We are pleased that this donation will help us continue our mission, which is to link our region's food bounty with those in the area who cannot provide for themselves," said Frank Schmidt, executive director of the Fonda Food Bank. Martha Redler, president of the Acme Foundation, added, "We have seen firsthand the contribution this organization makes to our community and are pleased to be in a position to help the Food Bank expand its reach to even more needy people."

Founded by Joseph J. Acme in 1948, the Acme Foundation is Fonda's oldest foundation. It provides funding for programs that help the poor and the elderly.

The Fonda Food Bank provides food to those who need it most. This year, the Food Bank will solicit and distribute more than one million pounds of food to thousands of individuals through senior centers, after school programs, and soup kitchens.

# # #

Use this worksheet to help you begin writing a press release. After you fill in the blanks, write the release, making sure your news is in the beginning and that information and paragraphs flow in a logical progression. The most important information comes first, followed by the least important information. (A worksheet that can be photocopied is included in the Appendix.)

News Release Writing Worksheet

FOR IMMEDIATE RELEASE (or Release Date)

Most releases can be used immediately. If that's the case, write FOR IMMEDIATE RELEASE. If the information can't be used before a specific date or time, it's FOR RELEASE (INSERT DATE AND TIME). What's your situation?

Contact name, phone number, and e-mail address.

Who should get calls from reporters?

_____

_____

_____

Attention-getting headline

Announce the release subject with active verbs and colorful words.

_____

Lead paragraph

Summarize your news in one sentence. Add a second sentence with a few more details. Read them over—do they say what they should? Make sure the sentences aren't too long.

_____

_____

_____

Five *Ws* and One *H*

Who, what, when, where, why, and how? You might have answered some of these questions in the lead paragraph. Answer the rest in the next two or three paragraphs.

_____

_____

_____

Quote

Does this release warrant a quote? Who is being quoted? What is the gist of that person's comments?

_____

_____

_____

Paragraph about your company

Conclude your release with a boilerplate paragraph that summarizes what your organization does.

_____

_____

_____

GET APPROVAL

Before sending the release out, make sure it is approved by the appropriate people internally (and externally, in situations where you've quoted people outside the organization, as we have with our example). This gives you one last opportunity to make sure you have your facts straight, which protects both you and your organization. It also eliminates surprises. (Do you really want your executive director to see her quote for the first time while enjoying her morning coffee?) When it comes to media materials, always err on the side of caution when it comes to material review and approval.

DOS AND DON'TS

Here are a few additional guidelines to help you produce the best news release possible.

- *Do* type your release with double-spacing.
- *Don't* use all capital letters.
- *Don't* worry about your writing skills. Yes, you want your news release to be as well written as possible. But if you've got a good story, you've used complete sentences, and you've presented the key facts in the proper order—most to least important—your story will be considered even if you don't know whether to use *that* or *which*.
- *Do* double-check all name spellings and proofread carefully.
- *Don't* rely on your computer's spellchecker. When in doubt, use a dictionary. If your spelling is so bad that you're never in doubt, have a colleague proofread it.
- *Do* ask a colleague to review your release for grammar and style, too.
- *Do* purchase a journalism style book such as *The Associated Press Stylebook and Briefing on Media Law* so that your press release mimics newspaper and magazine style. Style details such as proper capitalization make a difference to the busy reporter who doesn't have time to change improper job title capitalization. You'll find

colleagues resisting the accepted journalism style, but stand firm, using the style book as your ally.

- *Do* compare your news releases to what runs in the paper to see how your original compares with the final version. Learn from the changes.
- *Don't* use superlatives and exclamation marks. They're the mark of an amateur. You're too good for that.
- *Do* keep it short, to no more than 400 words.

HOW TO WRITE A TIP SHEET

As noted, tip sheets are news releases that offer advice or tips. Remember, they can be "evergreen"—usable any time—or linked to seasonal situations. Any organization can easily create one simply by tapping into the knowledge of its many experts. Ball State University garners publicity for its Teachers College by distributing tip sheets on topics that will guide parents as they help their children learn. The school's tip sheets have offered parents advice from one professor on finding ways to read to children in the morning and tips from another on how to deal with the good, the bad, and the ugly report cards (see the example in the Appendix). The beauty of tip sheets is that the content can be reused. The tips offered in a news release can be repackaged into a small booklet or brochure or another handout, they can be available on the organization's Web site so they're accessible to anyone seeking that type of information, and they can appear in the marketing newsletter sent to donors and others.

Use a tip sheet to generate short column notes in a newspaper or magazine or to interest a reporter, editor, or producer in a feature article or talk show interview on the tip sheet topic. Here's how to create an effective tip sheet.

Use a News Release Format

Use a news release format. The biggest difference between a tip sheet and a traditional press release is that the body of the tip sheet includes your tips or advice in a numbered or bulleted format. Start with a headline that mimics those on magazine covers—"Five ways to lose weight before June" or "Top seven mistakes shoppers make." Here's the headline used by the Ball State publicist on the morning reading tip sheet: "Reading should be a part of a well-balanced breakfast."

Write your first paragraph so it explains why the tips are necessary. The first paragraph and introductory text for the morning reading tip sheet was:

> "Two scoops of reading in the morning will improve children's literacy," says one Ball State University education expert. "Adjusting schedules to add reading time before or after breakfast will allow parents to make use of time when children are ready to learn rather than fall asleep," says Claudia McVicker, an assistant professor of elementary education in Ball State's Teachers College.

Notice how the writer introduced the expert and presented her credentials. You can also do this in the second paragraph, when you present a quotation. This should provide more detail about why the tip sheet is necessary. Here's the second paragraph in the morning reading tip sheet:

> "Children learn best in the morning, and a child's response to a book helps comprehension," she said. "If you read to soothe your child to sleep, you may not see her hop like the frog when you read, 'Jump, Frog, Jump!' or hear him chime in when you read 'Chicka Chicka Boom Boom.'"

Set up your tips with a sentence or a short paragraph, as we have here:

> McVicker offers the following hints to squeeze some reading into morning routines:

Then list your tips with bullets or numbers. When tips are listed this way, rather than in traditional paragraphs, editors can quickly scan them to see if they would be useful to readers—or not. Make sure you write your tips in an active voice with strong verbs. And make sure they provide advice, not reasons to do something or product features. Here are a few of the tips in the reading release so you can get a sense of how this works.

- *School lunch literacy.* Post the school lunch list on the fridge and read the lunch menu with your children every day. After several weeks, they will know the days of the week and will recognize many new words.
- *Cereal spelling.* Buy some Alphabits cereal and spell some words on the table for your children to read when they get to the table. They will look forward to the message each morning.
- *Shaving cream literacy.* While dads are shaving, they can put a small dollop of shaving cream on the bathroom counter and dictate letters or words for children to write with their fingers.

Finally, add the concluding boilerplate paragraph that you put on most press releases. Here's the paragraph for the morning reading tip sheet:

> Ball State University, located in Muncie, Ind., is the third-largest public university in Indiana, with more than 18,000 students. Originally a private teacher training school when it opened in 1899, Ball State became a university in 1965. Ball State, with its 1,035-acre campus, has many nationally ranked programs and highly touted immersion-learning experiences.

If you're struggling for tip sheet ideas, ask the people on the front lines what they know the most about and what topics people ask questions about over and over. Drawing from their knowledge as practitioners and from inquiries received by the people you serve will give you an excellent starting point. Think in terms of seasonal issues affecting your field, as well.

Once you have a solid idea, use the Tip Sheet Writing Worksheet to help you get started (a worksheet that can be photocopied is included in the Appendix). After you fill in the blanks on the worksheet, write the tip sheet, making certain it reads smoothly.

Holiday **T**ips **S**core for **O**nline **R**eligion **R**esource

InterfaithFamily.com provides a number of services to families whose members come from different religious backgrounds. A perennial topic of interest is the stress and tension that can occur during the holidays. The organization helps individuals whose partner or spouse has a different religious background cope in this situation by distributing tip sheets through the media, allowing for a broader reach. Topics have included how to help children understand that their grandparents on their father's side of the family celebrate different holidays or how to establish a family's own traditions for the holidays. They've also combined the tip sheets with survey results. For the "December Dilemma," when Jews in interfaith families may feel uncomfortable with a Christmas tree, InterfaithFamily conducted a survey about attitudes and offered solutions through tips. The survey tip sheet was used in a wide range of daily newspapers nationwide, from California to Massachusetts.

Tip Sheet Writing Worksheet

FOR IMMEDIATE RELEASE (or Release Date)

Most tip sheets can be used immediately. If that's the case, write FOR IMMEDIATE RELEASE. If the information can't be used before a specific date or time, it's FOR RELEASE (INSERT DATE AND TIME).

What's your situation?

_____

Contact name, phone number, and e-mail address

Who should get calls from reporters?

_____

_____

_____

Attention-getting headline

Include the number of tips—"Five Ways to . . ." or "Ten Tips for . . . ." Use active, colorful words.

_____

Lead paragraph

What's the situation? Why is this advice necessary?

_____

_____

_____

The expert

Who is the expert (name, title, any other necessary credentials)?

_____

Quote

What does the expert offering the tips have to say about the subject?

_____

_____

_____

The tips

Use bullets or numbers when listing the tips in punchy, pithy, how-to language.

1. Tip
2. Tip
3. Tip
4. Tip
5. Tip
6. Tip
7. Tip
8. Tip
9. Tip
10. Tip

Paragraph about your company

Conclude your tip sheet with a boilerplate paragraph that summarizes what your organization does.

_____

_____

_____

E-MAIL, FAX, OR U.S. MAIL?

Send your news release via the recipient's preferred format. When you don't know what that is, use your own preferred format. If sending via e-mail, give thought to your subject line. If your headline is short enough, use that. If it's too long, shorten it. Don't use "press release" or "news release," though. Such subject lines are too generic and might get your message deleted unread. If you're faxing the release, make sure you include a cover sheet with the recipient's name. As for the U.S. mail, while more and more communicators are using e-mail to reach reporters, it's still acceptable to use regular mail. In fact, some reporters prefer snail mail. It saves them the step of printing out your information. Make sure, though, when faxing or mailing to include a note at the end of the release that indicates you can e-mail the text to the recipient so the release doesn't have to be retyped.

NEXT STEPS

Before moving on to the next chapter about pitch letters, take time to do the following:

- Make a list of what's newsworthy in your organization.
- Use that list to create another one—a list of press releases you might write and distribute in the next four months.
- Create a list of tip sheet topics from your own knowledge of your organization.
- Expand the tip sheet list by talking with others to learn more from their experiences.

7

HOW WILL YOU SAY IT
IN A PITCH LETTER

Less experienced publicists often confuse a news release with a story pitch, but they are different animals. A news release announces news. Sometimes there's a larger story in that announcement, but many times there isn't. Quite often, that news release generates only a short news item. That's all that's needed; that's all that's appropriate. So don't expect a major feature article or a talk show segment to follow after you send a media contact a news release and nothing more.

If you want to generate an article or a talk show interview, use a pitch letter. As noted briefly in Chapter 5, a pitch letter tells the media gatekeeper about the idea, why it's important, and why the outlet's audience will be interested. Even if you've pitched your idea on the phone, chances are you'll need to follow up on the idea with a letter. In this chapter, you'll learn how to do it successfully.

KNOW YOUR TARGET

Take the time to study the media outlet or outlets you're targeting. It is essential that you know what they use and don't use. If you don't, you'll likely be wasting your time and theirs—and media gatekeepers quickly ignore time-wasting pitchers. You don't always get a second chance. For print, read back issues to determine which section of the newspaper or magazine is the best fit for your idea. When pitching local TV, watch the various talk shows to determine if your interview idea would fit best for a morning news program or a weekend public affairs show. Understanding how or where the outlet might use your idea helps you customize your pitch so that it meets that particular outlet's needs. This means that, even when pitching multiple outlets as part of a campaign, you need to tailor your basic letter for each outlet.

Make sure you send your letter to the appropriate contact by name as well as title. As noted in Chapter 4, if you aren't certain whom to contact, call the outlet and ask. They're happy to share that information, so don't be shy about asking for it.

Don't get too uptight when writing your letter. Too many of us fall back into our college English essay mode when writing letters to anyone but our parents or friends because we're trying to hard to impress. The goal in any business writing is not to impress but to communicate clearly and effectively.

Pitch Produces for Pajama Program

The Pajama Program, a national children's charity that provides new pajamas to needy and abused youngsters, has found e-mailed pitch letters to be especially effective in raising awareness and generating financial and clothing donations. The Boreland Group, Inc., which does pro bono PR for the charity, uses a straightforward message subject line—"Story Concept: Pajama Program"—so the recipient knows it's a pitch. The first line secures interest: "When you were a child, did you go to bed naked?" The letter (see Appendix) then explains how the Program makes sure that underprivileged children can sleep in new, clean pajamas instead of street clothes, underwear, or nothing at all. Publicity in Oprah Winfrey's magazine and in many other media outlets has allowed the organization to collect and donate more than 20,000 pairs of pj's to disadvantaged youngsters. While helping the Pajama Program achieve its goal, the placements ensure that thousands of children go to bed each night in fresh, clean pajamas, knowing that someone cares about them.

The best thing to do when writing media materials is forget everything you learned about writing while pulling an all-nighter on that essay about the symbolism in Charles Dickens's *Bleak House*. College writing is academic. Media writing is conversational and friendly. Write your pitch letter as if you were explaining the situation to that neighbor we referred to earlier, but make sure you select a neighbor who doesn't have a Ph.D. in cellular biology. What would she want to know about this idea? Tell her in clear and simple language that is devoid of your field's buzzwords and acronyms. Don't refer to aggregation, bloatware, or interdisciplinary learning. Your readers will lose interest before they can find their secret buzzword decoder rings.

THE FORMULA

Your goal is to communicate your story or segment idea clearly and convincingly. You want the reader to say, "This is a great idea!" To do that, your letter needs a logical flow of relevant information, all packaged into one page or less. Nobody will place a curse on you if it's longer than that, but in today's short attention span world, it's hard to hold the reader's interest for more than one page of information. You want to sell the readers before their attention wanders. Here are the key elements to include:

- Show that you've studied the media outlet.
- Start with an attention-getting first paragraph.
- Support your idea with research or statistics that show how serious or important this issue is.
- If you're pitching TV, indicate how the story is visual.
- Include suggestions for other information sources.
- Explain why an interview with your organization/spokesperson is essential to the story. List their credentials. If your pitch letter is for a bylined article that you would write, explain why you are the best person to write the article. If you've written articles before, say so.
- Include supporting materials when necessary or possible.
- Conclude by saying that you will call soon to determine interest.

Let's take a look at these elements individually.

Show You Know the Outlet

It's often possible to show you know the media outlet up front: "I've noticed that the Living section has increased its coverage of environmental issues. Here's an article idea on an important environmental topic that you haven't covered yet but that your readers will be interested in." This lead-in will "warm up" the letter reader, who will appreciate the fact that you understand the newspaper's editorial content. You can also do this after your attention-getting lead paragraph by writing, "This is an important issue for your readers, and I've noticed that, while you've increased coverage of environmental issues, you haven't addressed this topic yet. I'd like to help you do that."

Get Attention at the Beginning

You want to grab the reader's attention with the first paragraph describing the story. This is the most important part of the letter, so take time to get it right. There are a number of ways to do this; the one you choose depends on your topic and writing experience. Here are some common and effective ways to do this.

Use a straightforward approach. This approach is easiest for people who don't write these letters regularly. "I'm writing to suggest you write an article about . . . ." or, "I'm writing to suggest you interview . . . about this topic . . . ." It's a nice, clean way to get to the point quickly. However, if you like a challenge and want to try something more creative, consider the following alternatives.

Put a face on the issue with an anecdote. *The Wall Street Journal* starts every front page, center column article with one individual's story. This very effective method humanizes the topic, making it easier for readers to relate to it.

Startle the reader with a shocking statistic or fact. This helps us see how bad the problem really is. When pitching locally, rather than nationally, use local statistics in addition to national figures when you can get them. A reporter is going to say, "Sure, that's a problem nationally, but what's the situation here?" You want to answer that question before it's asked.

Ask a question to which almost any reader could relate. It needs to be a question the reader probably can't answer, though, for this to work effectively. When the Terri Schiavo life support case was making headlines, a letter proposing an article to a male editor on how to handle advance care planning about end-of-life care might have started with, "If your wife was very seriously injured or ill and couldn't communicate her wishes, would you know what kind of care she would want? Would she want to be resuscitated if her heart stopped? Would she want a feeding tube if there was no brain activity?"

Use Statistics for Support

Statistics help make your case. It's one thing to say that American students don't know enough about history; it's another thing to prove this with statistics that might also shock or surprise us. The statistics can come from anywhere, as long as they're relevant and credible. A good way to find what you need is with a Google search. For example, typing in *survey students history "lack of knowledge"* will turn up a link to a report revealing that 65 percent of college seniors surveyed failed to pass a high school-level American history test. National organizations are another excellent source of research results, whether you're part of that organization or not. These include groups like the Alzheimer's Association, which address specific health issues, as well as medical specialty and other trade associations. There's a national group for a surprising number of topics, and many of them do research. Check their Web sites for topic fact sheets or contact their media relations departments for help.

Highlight TV Visuals

Pitch letters are used with television to generate talk show interviews and special event coverage. Television relies on visuals. They are essential for on-site news coverage, but they're also used during one-on-one talk show interviews in the studio. When you're enticing a news assignment editor to send a reporter and photographer to a live event, describe what they can expect to see there. What's visually exciting? What activities will be going on? For an in-studio talk show interview, let the producer know if you have props that will enhance the interview. If you have video footage they can use—referred to in the industry as "B roll"—say so in your letter.

Suggest Other Sources

Here's the deal with successful pitching: the more you help the journalist do the job, the more successful you'll be (as long as your idea is good). So always, always, always do some subject research before pitching so you can save that gatekeeper time and frustration by providing the resources needed to develop a well-rounded story.

Print reporters always use multiple sources for features. How do you figure out what sources to offer? First, study a few recent feature articles in that publication. You'll see that they usually try to offer a balanced perspective—maybe there's good news along with the bad news. Or maybe it's bad news, so the article offers some possible solutions. You'll also discover that feature articles require many different information sources, often both local and national. You want to help, particularly with the local sources, so that when possible, you can steer the reporter away from your direct competition and towards another group that works collaboratively with you.

If your organization provides shelter for the homeless and you're pitching a story about how your city has far more homeless people than most realize, and how the problem is getting worse and not better, you'll want to help the reporter identify whom else to interview. Here's a potential list of resources for your pitch—and this is just a start:

- Two or three currently or formerly homeless people who have agreed to talk with a reporter (without "real" people to interview, you won't have a story). You don't need names for the letter—all you have to do is state that you have people ready to talk
- A local soup kitchen

- A national expert on the subject, perhaps a college professor or book author, who does not have to be local
- A national organization that works to help reduce or eliminate the problem and can offer potential solutions

You know better than anyone in your community who the leaders are on your topic. Help make them available to the reporter without being asked. You'll bring yourself closer to publicity success.

Make Your Organization Essential to the Story

Why or how is your organization essential to this story? Perhaps you're the only organization serving this population or tackling this issue. Maybe you're the largest. Maybe you're the smallest, but you just won an impressive award for accomplishing so much despite your size. Establish your credentials so it's clear that this story can't be told without your voice.

The Campaign with a Heart

Wanger Associates publicized the 50th anniversary of the National Heart, Lung, and Blood Institute's Framingham Heart Study with a personalized pitch letter focusing on the study's importance to the health of Americans and the availability of multigenerational families from the study for interviews. The letter was attached to a press kit that included a news release, a timeline of major study findings, an overview of the most important current projects, a list of top experts in the field, and contact information for key scientists involved in the study. The resulting *U.S. News & World Report* cover story and more than 50 individual feature stories appearing in more than 1,000 media outlets generated increased awareness of the ongoing significance of the study and honored the citizens of Framingham, Massachusetts, who have participated for five decades.

Include Supporting Materials

One page single-spaced isn't much room to tell everything you know about the subject, is it? That's okay. That's what attachments are for. Along with your pitch, send a news release, backgrounder, fact sheet, photos, other news articles—anything that helps support your case that this is a good story or segment idea. Don't go overboard, but if you have good supporting documents, definitely include them. The pitch about the homeless, for example, might include a fact sheet with statistics about the area's homeless population—how many, ages, what services are available to them, and so on. Or it might include nothing more than a photo of a packed-to-the-gills shelter. What information do you have that can help tell or sell the story? That's what you should include.

Who Will Do What Next?

Always conclude with a statement that explains the next step. Avoid the passive approach—"Please call me if you're interested." Be aggressive and positive: "I'll call you at the end of the week to determine your interest in this idea. I look forward to working with you on it."

HIT THE SEND BUTTON

When submitting via e-mail, give some thought to the subject line. Indicate that your message contains an article idea and include a short reference to the subject. For the article on the city's homeless it might be: "Article idea: Dramatic increase in area homeless." Try to keep it short and interesting.

Before you send your letter, try this trick: e-mail it to yourself first and read it as an e-mail message. This technique will help you catch glitches you missed before. When you're satisfied with the message, you can send it via e-mail, fax, or regular mail. Typically, the method you use depends on the media contact's preferences (which you've researched and logged in your media database, right?). The one exception is situations where you have several attachments. In those cases, use regular mail.

NEXT STEPS

Before moving on to the next chapter about publicity tactics and how to use them, take time to do the following:

- List three article or talk show segment ideas you'd like to pitch.
- Brainstorm the best way to present each idea.
- Begin thinking about other information or interview resources for each of the ideas.

Part Three

TACTICS

8

WHEN WILL YOU SAY IT? PUBLICITY WITHOUT AN EVENT

Here's where you discover how to become more opportunistic, looking for publicity possibilities others might overlook—and miss. You'll learn more about which tools work best in certain situations, how to pitch to different types of media outlets, and how to bring to life those great newsworthy ideas you generated after reading Chapter 2. You'll also discover how to become more aggressive through editorial briefings and by making certain you have a Web site that works hard for you in the background. Combine all of this essential information with tips for telephone pitching, and you've got everything you need to make a media splash on a regular basis with a small budget.

TOOLS AND OUTLETS

When pitching journalists with all the good ideas you're developing, it helps to know how they work, which methods and tools work best with which medium, and their deadlines. Some publicity tools are more useful in certain situations than in others. In general, the news release is useful with all types of media outlets because it is a recognized format for news announcements. This applies to tip sheets, too, because so much media information offers us advice we can use to do something better or faster. Longer pitch letters work best when communicating an article or talk show segment idea; shorter pitches are effective when you've got an idea to share with a media contact you know already or when pitching an idea to an e-newsletter editor.

Press kits are helpful to print reporters looking for depth and detail but less so with broadcast outlets. Radio producers would rather see a short news release, a surprising fact sheet, and a list of suggested questions. TV news assignment editors need just a news release, a media alert, a brief pitch letter with a great idea, or a fact sheet—whatever has the key facts and information without a lot of background information.

Print outlets emphasize topic knowledge, because newspapers and magazines have room to explore a subject in greater depth than certain other outlets. Half-hour radio or TV public affairs talk shows also need this depth. But television news and drive-time radio show hosts need knowledge as well as someone who can engage viewers and listeners with an animated, energetic personality. This is because for some reason, television makes people look less dynamic and energetic—even flamenco guitarist and actress Charo (cuchi-cuchi!) has to ratchet it up a notch when she's on TV. And a low-key personality on radio will put drivers to sleep. Use this information to decide if you need one spokesperson for print and another for broadcast interviews. Here's a more complete breakdown by media type.

Newspapers

Daily and weekly newspapers have as many differences as similarities. The differences start with the obvious—deadlines and the volume of information needed each week. With dailies, the paper's deadline depends on whether it's a morning or an afternoon publication. The news deadline for a morning paper is early evening, while for afternoon papers it's early morning. When pitching stories that aren't breaking news, what's more relevant is "worst time to call." Avoid calling morning paper reporters late in the afternoon, when they might be on deadline. Avoid calling afternoon paper reporters early in the morning. The worst time to call a weekly newspaper depends on its publication date. Typically, that's two days before the publication date, so if your paper publishes on a Friday, don't call on Wednesday. The best day to call is one day before publication date—in this example, Thursday. That week's paper has been put to bed, and reporters are lining up their story ideas for the following week.

Deadlines also apply to when you want your news to appear in print. Try to contact a daily with your feature idea about three weeks before you want it to appear. That gives the reporter enough time to get approval, line up interviews, and execute the assignment. Contact a weekly newspaper about four weeks before you'd like the publicity to appear to make sure your area's reporter can fit it into a busy schedule filled with town board meetings, school events, and other local activities.

Daily newspapers use more material than weekly newspapers, but the weekly is an easier publication to pitch if you've got a local story. Don't waste a weekly reporter's time with a story idea that doesn't have a local connection, but when you do have a good idea with that essential local element, expect a warm reception. Because they are often understaffed, weeklies are also more likely to use news releases as you've written them, which can be a plus because you know the information you want to be used *will* be used. Weeklies are also more likely to accept "submitted" photos rather than shooting their own.

Monthly Magazines

Magazines are published with deadlines of anywhere from one to five or six months ahead of time, but three months' lead time is typical. Local magazines have a shorter cycle than national magazines; with national publications, allow a minimum of four months. A publicity plan that includes magazines with other outlets often has a timeline that involves releasing news to magazines months before releasing it to daily news outlets.

Because magazines publish less frequently than newspapers, it is harder to place a magazine story—there's just less room for the good ideas. In addition, national magazines receive pitches from people like you all over the country—so they have less room but receive more ideas. The competition is stiff. In general, trade and local magazines are easier to get into if your idea is good.

Electronic Newsletters

Because each has a different publication frequency and production schedule, ask the editor of the e-newsletter or e-zine you're targeting about deadlines. While some are distributed as soon as they're written, others go through a design process that makes distribution slightly less immediate. The best way to communicate with an e-newsletter is through e-mail.

Local TV News

Contact TV news staffers by e-mail, fax, or phone. Most have their news department contact information on their Web sites. While it's recommended that you send your information to the assignment editor, it's okay to contact a reporter directly when you have a relationship with that person, when you know that person supports your cause or organization, or when you know that reporter covers your topic specifically, as is the case with a medical or health reporter.

Most news department staffers working on the 5:00 or 6:00 PM and the 10:00 or 11:00 PM newscasts are at work by 9:30 AM. Shortly thereafter, they have a morning news meeting to decide the stories for the late afternoon broadcast. There's a second news meeting in the afternoon, when the department assigns the stories for the late evening newscast. This means you want them to have your information in hand at least the day before you want the story to run, so send it several days in advance and follow up the day before you want the coverage. The assignment editor then has enough information to decide at the meeting that your story is worth covering.

If you want to be a guest on the chat portion of the early morning news shows that air before the 7:00 AM network news programs, such as *Good Morning America,* or on a noon news program, call to pitch at 9:30 AM—30 minutes after the show goes off the air—to catch the producer before they go home. The producer will tell you if that's a good time to talk or if they have another preference.

Radio

As discussed earlier in the book, it's hard to get the attention of radio news departments. Most opportunities will come through drive-time or talk show interviews, with all-talk stations offering the most potential. If you are your organization's spokesperson and will be the person interviewed, the best thing to do is to pitch yourself over the telephone to the show's producer. This lets the producer hear how you handle yourself—do you sound energetic? Can you be engaging? Radio is all about sound.

It's possible, though, that you will be pitching someone else as a guest. This happens all the time and will present no problems, especially if you prepare your spokesperson well for the interview (see Chapter 10). If the producer likes your idea and wants more information, fax or mail a press kit that includes a pitch letter for the idea that indicates your stand or position on the issue being discussed. Include a list of sample questions in the order in which you want them asked. This is important because interviewers often don't have time to get smart on your topic, so this helps them get up to speed quickly. If you've got press clippings on the topic, include them.

Pitch talk show producers unless the station is small enough that the hosts book their own guests. Log all of your calls in your media database, or you'll lose track of the details and status. Call morning show producers within one hour of the end of the talk show—for example, if it runs from 6:00 to 10:00 AM, call between 10:00 and 11:00 AM. Call afternoon show producers an hour before or after the start/finish of the show. In all cases, don't call when the show is on the air. When you get voicemail, leave a short message with your phone number. Keep following up until you reach the producer, then present a quick pitch that you have practiced beforehand.

GETTING OPPORTUNISTIC AND AGGRESSIVE

Chapter 2 showed how to create news when you don't have any, but we didn't address what to do with the results of your creativity. Here's how to use and apply those publicity tools to generate media coverage when you're not using an attention-getting special event (discussed in Chapter 9) to help secure publicity. The various opportunistic, nonevent approaches proposed in Chapter 2 include commenting on national headline news, tapping into TV storylines, doing a survey, creating a list, taking advantage of newsworthy seasons and holidays, and hosting a contest or competition (without an event). Now that you understand each opportunity, here's the information you need to capitalize on each.

Headline News

When you're commenting on national headline news, you have to respond immediately in the most aggressive way possible. Use the phone instead of e-mail, because you don't know how often the media contact checks for e-mail messages and you don't want your information to sit in an in-box too long. Call the appropriate media contact—probably the TV news assignment editor or a reporter or editor at a daily newspaper—and say, "I'm so-and-so and I have a local angle on a current national story. The story is . . . and the local connection is. . . ."

If they're interested, they'll ask you to fax or e-mail any additional information they might need. Even if they schedule an interview but don't ask for background material, send a fact sheet or backgrounder on your organization and your spokesperson's bio anyway so you are identified properly in the interview. (If you don't provide that in writing, you can't be certain they'll get it right.) When interviewed in person, provide the interviewer with another copy of that background information. The reporter will appreciate your attention to factual details. It makes the reporter's job a little easier, and that's one of your goals.

TV Storylines

Tapping into TV storylines can take you down two productive paths—one, with the news department of the network affiliate airing the show and the other, with the op-ed section of your newspaper. With TV news departments, you're offering a local connection to an important issue addressed on a national television show. With the editorial page of the newspaper, you're providing your organization's opinion or advice on the subject, linking it back to the show. If you know days in advance that a soap opera, a TV drama, a TV news magazine, or a sitcom will be addressing your organization's issue, you can use e-mail or the fax machine to begin the communication process with TV news assignment editors and editorial page editors. If you found out this morning that the show is running tonight, pick up the phone.

When contacting the TV news assignment editor, explain that a popular show on that network will include a storyline about an important issue that your organization addresses on a routine basis. You'd like to offer your spokesperson for an interview with the local perspective on the issue for the late evening newscast following the television show.

While it would help to know how the show is going to handle your issue, it's impossible to know this in advance (unless the show is a rerun). That won't stop you from telling a reporter what local viewers need to know about the subject.

Your pitch to the editorial page editor is similar, but instead of an interview, you're offering to supply the newspaper with an op-ed to run either the day of the program or the day or two after. The downside of providing an op-ed before the show airs is that you can't be certain how your topic will be handled on the show until you see it. That means your essay will have to address the issue in a general way, making just a reference to the fact that it will be one of the storylines on the show airing that night. You will not be able to counter any misinformation that might have been presented in the show—or applaud its accuracy—but you will have a timely opportunity to present your perspective.

The ideal situation is an essay that runs soon after the show airs. TV program airing times and newspaper publication deadlines might make it difficult for your essay to appear the next morning, but two days later isn't impossible. Use your essay to congratulate the producers on calling national attention to such an important issue, explain why it is important, and underscore or correct information presented in the show. Conclude with a call to action—what can readers do to help?

Surveys

Whom you survey depends on the topic and what you want to do with it. You might want to survey just members or constituents, or you might need to query the general public. Whether or not you need to engage the services of a professional for this project depends on its scope and how you plan to use the results.

For a survey designed to generate publicity in a local area only, you can do it yourself as long as you are thoughtful and careful about the questions asked. If you're surveying moviegoers about how they feel about violence in movies, you don't want to showcase your bias by asking, "Don't you agree that there's way too much violence in movies?" Take a more neutral stance, asking "Do you believe there's too much violence in movies?" Consider consulting with a professional to make certain your questions elicit the information you want and that you obtain a representative sampling.

There are a number of ways to conduct surveys. Organizations with a strong online community can use the free tools offered at Survey-Monkey (http://www.surveymonkey.com). Face-to-face questioning and paper forms work well, too. Keep the survey very short—just a few questions—to make it easier for people to respond and for you to tabulate and analyze the results.

Put your survey results into a news release that includes an appropriate headline, reports the survey results in the first paragraph, includes a strong quote from your spokesperson, suggests how your organization will use the information (if appropriate); and concludes with the boilerplate paragraph about your organization. Send it to all outlets in your media database, because this information might be as interesting to radio news directors as to newspaper reporters or TV assignment editors. Add it to your media relations toolkit, too, attaching the survey results release to pitch letters when it makes sense or to a press kit you might develop later. In addition to being used to generate news, it is also valuable background information for future media contacts.

Announce the survey results in your internal and external newsletters and on your Web site, as well. Your staff and constituents will be just as interested in this information as the general public.

Lists

Lists require less research but more creativity than a survey. Begin by brainstorming topics that are newsworthy and relevant to your current agenda. Perhaps you want to alert people to a frightening trend that needs to be addressed. A hospital might produce a list of the "top ten causes for emergency room visits" with advice on how to prevent some of those trips, while a group advocating pet adoptions might present the "top seven reasons why people leave animals at the shelter" with commentary about how to avoid unwanted pets.

Format your release like a tip sheet to announce your list. The title of the list makes a good release title—"Mercy Hospital Announces Top Ten Reasons for Emergency Room Visit; Offers Prevention Advice." Use the first paragraph simply to state that you have tabulated a list and why. It might read, "Emergency room visits have spiked recently, with Mercy Hospital seeing a 20 percent increase over last month. Here are the top 10 reasons people visit emergency rooms and how to prevent some of those visits." List your reasons in a numbered list format. Follow that with a strong quote from your spokesperson about why the hospital is addressing this topic. Follow that with advice in either paragraph or bulleted form, whichever seems most appropriate. Conclude with the boilerplate paragraph about your organization. It's not always necessary or appropriate to offer advice in a list release, but if it seems like a good idea, don't miss the opportunity to do so.

Send it to all outlets in your media database; add it to your media relations toolkit, too, so you can use it later as supporting information. As you would with a survey release, publish your list in your internal and external newsletters and on your Web site, too. (Always look for ways to get even more mileage from your press materials.)

Seasons and Holidays

As mentioned in Chapter 2, seasons and holidays are practically begging us to use them for publicity purposes. Use them to pitch an article idea, propose a talk show interview, or send a tip sheet. Start your brainstorming process by making two lists. On one list, write what's seasonal, if anything, about your organization's work. Are you busier some months than others? Is this predictable; if so, why? Add to that list any national day, week, or month that relates to your cause. If you're not aware of any, use *Chase's Calendar of Events* in the reference section of your library or Google your topic and the word *month*. Googling *food allergy annual month*, for example, yields a Food Allergy Awareness Week in May.

On your second list, write down all the seasonal news stories you can remember seeing or hearing. (The list in Chapter 2 is a good start.) Ask other people for their input. Compare the two lists—is there overlap you can capitalize on? Food Allergy Awareness Week in May probably coincides with a seasonal allergy story. Use that to your advantage with a story pitch that begins with:

> While most people are thinking about seasonal allergies requiring antihistamines at this time of the year, others have food allergies on their mind. May 10-16 is Food Allergy Awareness Week, reminding us of the 7 million Americans with food allergies and the problems they face *all* year.

Use the two lists you've created to come up with a third list of seasonal or holiday stories you can pitch and contribute to.

You can use these ideas as the basis for pitch letters, news releases, or tip sheets. A news release is appropriate if you're using your seasonal tie-in to make an announcement, such as a schedule of local activities celebrating Food Allergy Awareness Week. Use a tip sheet when you're providing advice or tips, following the guidelines outlined in Chapter 6. Depending on your idea, a seasonal or holiday tie-in could work for most outlets on your media distribution list.

Contests and Competitions

Contests that don't require an event are cost-effective and easy to execute. What can you have fun with? What's the most, biggest, greatest, best in your field? Sponsor a contest to find out. A Goodwill thrift store might sponsor a contest to find the ugliest bridesmaid's dress, while a literacy volunteer organization might seek nominations for the best book of the 20th century.

The beauty of contests is that they provide multiple publicity opportunities. You can make news when you announce the contest and later, when you announce the winner. Use a news release to make the announcement, being careful to write a great headline and include the specifics in the first two paragraphs. Important details you don't want to overlook include how people can enter (e-mail, from your Web site, fax, mail, or on-site); what's required for entries; and the entry deadline. Tell them how and when you'll select the winner and what the winner receives. Include a quote from your spokesperson about why you're hosting the contest, making certain the quote reflects the tone of the contest—

don't be stuffy if the contest isn't. Wrap it up with your boilerplate paragraph about the organization.

Send a second release announcing the winner. If your contest has good visuals—such as the winning ugliest bridesmaid's dress—send the release with a note inviting TV news departments and newspaper photographers to come to your facility to meet and interview the contest winner when you present the prize.

PITCHING BY TELEPHONE

Much of what you've read so far has given you newsworthy ideas to pitch on the phone. Let's be honest: while more and more of us are relying on e-mail for quick, convenient communication, there's no substitute for the telephone and the advantages of voice-to-voice communication. You can save yourself a lot of time by starting the pitching process with the phone. It gets you an instant response and it can provide feedback you can use to tweak your idea or for future encounters. Here are a few tips to help you overcome any phone-pitching phobia so that you can become as efficient as possible.

- *Start with the least important media outlet first.* That way, you're making mistakes where they hurt the least. Use that feedback to refine the pitch so it's perfect by the time you get to your top outlet.
- *Ask if it's a good time to talk.* No matter how much you know about deadlines, it's always possible to call at a bad time.
- *Prepare ahead of time.* Even veteran pitchers write out what they want to say so they communicate as clearly as possible. Practice saying it a few times so you're comfortable with it. If the language seems awkward when you speak it, rewrite it.
- *Keep it short.* Summarize your idea in no more than two sentences. Then ask, "Are you interested in this?"
- *Use a no response productively.* If your contact says, "No thanks," and seems friendly, use that opportunity to ask, for educational purposes, what would have improved the idea. Get feedback when you can and learn from it.
- *Never, ever argue.* Just don't. You might have just presented a Pulitzer-prize winning idea, but if the journalist passes on it, accept

the rejection gracefully and move on. Don't argue, don't go over the reporter's head, don't try again later "when they might be in a better mood." Drop it.

Publicity **D**ials **U**p **P**hone **S**ervice

Phones for Life (PFL), a charity that collects donated cell phones, programs them for one-touch 911 dialing, and distributes them to seniors, got a significant boost in phone donations and corporate sponsorships when volunteer publicist Kelly Kreth made a simple call to a single, but powerful, media outlet. Kreth contacted NY1, Manhattan's television news station, to nominate PFL president Ray Dorman as a "New Yorker of the Week." The award is given to people the station believes make a difference. The winners are profiled on the network. When Dorman was profiled, the on-screen exposure generated nearly 1,000 calls from people requesting a 911 cell phone or inquiring about how to donate one. Showing how publicity begets publicity, the TV broadcast led to articles in other media outlets including the *Los Angeles Times*, *American Medical News*, Long Island's *Newsday*, and other publications. In addition, since the NY1 profile, Canon has become the organization's first corporate sponsor.

WHAT ABOUT FOLLOW UP?

You've pitched a great idea and sent all the appropriate information, but your e-mail in-box hasn't chimed to announce the journalist's response and your phone isn't ringing with media calls, either. Do you follow up? And when does following up border on stalking? You should and you shouldn't follow up, depending on the situation. Don't bother to follow up a news release with a call or an e-mail message that says, "Did you get it?" While there's a chance the journalist didn't get it, the call is annoying. Who would get any work done if every person who sent a press release made a follow-up call? But with releases that are particularly important for whatever reason, it's okay to have an excuse to follow up that mailing—to offer a photo or to send a related article that might provide useful background information, for instance.

When you have something additional to offer, say just that: "I sent you a news release earlier this week on our new series of workshops for family caregivers. I have a good head shot of the workshop instructor—would you like me to e-mail it to you?" This gives the recipient an opportunity to say, "No thanks, we won't need it," or, "Yes, we might be able to use that with the item we're running on the workshops on Friday." With the first response, it's fine to ask, "That's good to know. Do you plan on using the release?" You'll get a yes, no, or maybe, and isn't that what you really want to know—whether it will be used, rather than if it was received? Note, too, that it's easier to have this dialog over the phone than through e-mail. The reporter can ignore you much more easily with e-mail, making the process far less productive for you.

While you don't want to follow up with every news release mailing, you do want to follow up article or talk show idea pitches, because if they aren't accepted at one outlet, you'll want to take them to another. Get that closure by making that phone call or sending that note. Get feedback if you can and use it to fine-tune the pitch before sending it elsewhere. On the other hand, if you've left three messages and had no response, feel free to move on. Don't call more than three times.

NEWSPAPER EDITORIAL BRIEFINGS

While these ideas can get your organization in the news, it's also possible to get great exposure through the editorial pages of a newspaper. The editorial section is very popular with newspaper readers, making it an important publicity target for nonprofit organizations. Chapter 5 explained how to place a guest essay or op-ed on these pages, but there's another way to secure this valuable real estate: convince the editorial board to take a stand on your issue and write about it in-house through an editorial page op-ed. Do this by getting a little aggressive and scheduling an editorial board meeting, a gathering of the editorial staff and invited guests. This is where you explore the issue, influence, educate, and answer questions. In the end, the board will evaluate the issue, decide if it wants to address it, and determine its position on the issue.

These meetings always include representatives of the editorial board—the people who write the editorials—and sometimes include reporters covering the general topic being discussed—the environment, education, religion, and so on. Having these beat reporters there helps you in two ways. First, you're talking with a well-informed reporter who is interested in learning more about the topic, and second, you might get a news story out of your meeting, too, if it would be appropriate. The groups are sometimes small and casual, sometimes larger and more formal. But they tend to get to get down to business pretty quickly. The editorial board wants to hear what you have to say.

Prepare Well First

Before scheduling a meeting, do some research. When narrowing your issue to a topic that's appropriate, keep in mind what newspapers like to have on their editorial pages. They want to tell readers more about those topics educated people might be discussing at a cocktail party or a neighborhood barbecue. For example, during the summer of 2005, people were talking about Tom Cruise's behavior after he fired his long-time publicist and hired his sister. Suddenly, normally private Cruise was out there with the media—*way* out there. While water cooler chatter initially centered on his behavioral changes, it soon moved in on a specific issue: Cruise's theory that postpartum depression could be cured with diet and exercise. Whether he's right or wrong, educated people were talking about this, making it a topic ripe for the editorial pages. It was a great opportunity for organizations working to help mothers with the problem.

You know your issue and your stance, but do you know how the newspaper has reported on it or related issues? If you don't, review six months worth of back issues, looking for articles on your issue or related topics. If you're advocating for stricter regulation of childcare providers, for example, find out what has been written on that subject already either as news—a bad situation at a day care center—or as a feature—perhaps how to find a good childcare provider. This will give you a sense of the paper's breadth or lack of knowledge of the subject—a rough knowledge benchmark.

At the same time, gather your own resources on the subject. Do you have everything you need to make a compelling case? Do you need to write a backgrounder or find that position paper from the National Association of Child Care Centers? Don't pick up the phone until you're confident you have the information you need to make your case.

Contact the Editorial Page Editor

To schedule a board meeting, call and ask the editorial page editor how to proceed (each newspaper has its own preferences). You will probably be asked to write a letter requesting an appointment. The newspaper might ask you to outline your position in your letter of request. If not, you'll want to do this anyway for the meeting, preparing a briefing sheet that informs while serving as an agenda.

Begin the briefing sheet by describing your issue in one or two sentences. Answer the question: what is the problem? Next, expand on the problem and the barriers to a solution in a way that is engaging, not academic. Use colorful descriptions. Then, explain why this is important to the readers. How will this help or hurt them? Use statistics if you can. Explain the impact of your issue. Finally, explain what you are doing about the issue and what others can do. Offer it as a handout at the meeting.

When your meeting is scheduled, get organized. Decide who will attend from your group, making certain that each person really should be there, either as the spokesperson or as somebody who can help answer questions. Don't bring people just to fill seats. Determine your spokesperson—most likely your executive director or your board chair. Your spokesperson is typically allowed 15 to 20 minutes to provide an overview and make a case. Prepare—but don't over-prepare—those remarks in advance. You might want to bring an outline but not a script. This is a conversation, not a Congressional testimony. You want to use a conversational tone, as if you're talking to neighbors.

The meeting usually begins with introductions. Your host may or may not elaborate on the newspaper's view on the subject, express interest in one particular aspect, or express a bias and ask you to comment on that position. Usually, however, your spokesperson is asked to make the presentation. This is followed by a question-and-answer period, but it's not unusual for board members to ask their questions as the spokesperson moves through the presentation. The end result is the same—a more informed editorial board. There might be questions your group can't answer. Promise to get the answers quickly, and make sure you know to whom to give the information.

While there's nothing wrong with asking at the meeting if the board will write an editorial, it's more likely that they will want to discuss the issue privately after you leave. Be certain to follow up to see if they need more information and to determine the decision.

PROFNET OFFERS NATIONAL OPPORTUNITIES

ProfNet is a tool that lets you be opportunistic in a more far-reaching way. This subscription service connects journalists with experts. Subscribers receive a collection of queries from reporters at magazines, newspapers, Web publications, and TV and radio programs delivered via e-mail several times a day. It is an excellent tool for any organization looking to raise its profile by appearing in national media outlets or local outlets in another region. It presents publicity opportunities you would never otherwise know about.

Here's how it works. Reporters use the journalists section of the ProfNet Web site to post a query for an article or segment. They describe the expert they need and why and provide an e-mail address or phone number for responses. Qualified sources respond with a brief summary of their credentials and how they might comment on the topic in an interview. The subscription rate for this service is $500 per year for nonprofit organizations (it's much higher for public relations firms). This price includes listings in ProfNet's experts database, a resource also used by journalists to search for biographical and contact information for experts by area of expertise; it's a more passive alternative to posting a query through the daily newsletter system. The fee also includes Profnet's leads, each a three-sentence story idea that summarizes your expert's perspective on a timely issue or trend. The leads get sent to 4,000 media outlets through ProfNet's daily delivery system.

This service lets you respond directly to journalists who state precisely the information they're looking for or to reach out quickly to comment on breaking news or a trend getting coverage. It offers nonprofit organizations an excellent opportunity to secure widespread media exposure. View the demonstration at http://www.profnet.com for more information.

RESPOND PROMPTLY TO INQUIRIES

If, after all this effort, a reporter calls with questions or wants an interview for a quote, respond promptly. Ask about the deadline, how much time is needed, and what the reporter is looking for in general so you can help your spokesperson prepare. Then make your spokesperson available according to the deadline, rearranging schedules if you have to, because if you don't, the journalist will find another organization to talk to. If the reporter is looking for background information, e-mail or fax it promptly. Then follow up to make sure it got there—technology isn't as reliable as we sometimes think.

NEXT STEPS

Before moving on to the next chapter explaining how to publicize an event, take time to do the following:

- Take the newsworthy ideas you developed after reading Chapter 2 and begin thinking about how to use them. Are they best used as article ideas or tip sheets? Are they good radio talk show interview topics or e-newsletter articles? Should one be a submitted op-ed or the subject of an editorial board meeting?
- Think about some of the other opportunities presented here and how they apply to your organization. Which are worth exploring further?

9

WHEN WILL YOU SAY IT? PUBLICIZING AN EVENT

Special events are common tactics in communications plans, because they can help an organization achieve a number of goals. They can help raise the organization's profile, shape or alter its image, generate contributions, attract volunteers or top employees—the list goes on. Special events cost money and are often time consuming to plan and execute, so make certain an event fits with your strategy and will help you reach your goals. Whenever possible, get enough grant funding or corporate sponsorships for your event to cover costs. As an alternative, try to become the beneficiary of an event hosted by another organization. In those situations, your primary responsibility is typically limited to supporting the event's marketing effort in exchange for the donation.

Here are just a few of the types of special events that can make news:

- Luncheon or dinner with celebrity keynote speaker
- Fundraising run or bike-a-thon
- Grand opening of a public facility, such as a museum or a zoo
- Creation of the world's biggest anything, with your organization as the event beneficiary

- Town hall meeting
- Golf tournament
- Community yard or garage sale
- Milestone anniversary
- Consumer or professional development conference
- Contest or competition with judges

INCORPORATE NEWSWORTHY ELEMENTS

To make sure your special event is as newsworthy as possible, incorporate elements that will help draw media attention. These include having a local media personality as an emcee, host, or honorary chair; a local media sponsor; good visuals for TV news; volunteer committees led by well-known people in the community; celebrity speakers from outside the community; participation by constituents who will benefit from the event and can help put a face on your cause; well-known honorees who will attract guests; and participation from civic, government, or industry leaders.

In addition, make sure you have several large signs on-site with your group's name and logo. On-site event signage ensures that your name will be included in the media coverage of the event in case the reporter doesn't mention it. Orchestrate on-site interviews so they are conducted in front of a logo banner. When appropriate for the type of event, have staffers and volunteers wear T-shirts printed with your name or logo in very large type. Some organizations opt for polo shirts, but the logos are too small to read on TV or in photos. Go for the maximum impact at the expense of fashion.

PUBLICIZE IN ADVANCE

Special events can't rely on publicity alone. They need to be promoted with a number of marketing tools besides publicity, including advertising, direct mail, e-mail, and word of mouth. Develop a plan and calendar that incorporates as many of these elements as you can afford. Advertising—and this is where a media sponsor who donates in-kind space or air time can make an impact—reaches out to those who aren't in your own marketing database. Use direct mail to reach people you know, using your in-house lists, and people you don't know by purchasing lists. Begin communicating with people you know well in advance of the event, keeping them informed of exciting developments—selection of the guest speaker or honorary chairperson—so they feel as though they're part of the planning process. Offer updates through e-mail, your marketing newsletter, and your Web site.

Publicity, because it can't be controlled or guaranteed, needs to supplement these methods. Work to get as much free media exposure as possible by publicizing the event in advance, on-site, and afterwards. What—and how much—you do depends on the nature of the event and the elements that are newsworthy, but you'll want to do certain things for all events. The first is to announce the event with a news release at the appropriate time, usually four to five weeks before the event (unless you're targeting monthly magazines, which will need it three to six months in advance). This gives everyone a heads-up. TV stations will file it for future use, while daily newspapers will start thinking about whether or how they might cover it.

Make sure the announcement release includes all relevant information—date, time, place, cost, deadline for ticket purchase or event registration, whom to contact for event information, special features, and so on. Send this to your standard media list but add the names of people who handle the calendar sections and newspaper photo editors, who might send a photographer. Notify your event contact person when the release is sent so the person is prepared for any resulting phone inquiries when the news gets used.

After the first release gets mailed, pitch any special feature article ideas related to the event so that they will appear in time to sell tickets or generate attendance. For example, the personal struggles of an individual associated with your cause allow a newspaper to tell that person's story in a way that includes information about your upcoming event, particularly if it's a fundraiser. National celebrities bring a different set of media relations opportunities that we'll discuss later.

If your event is highly visual, pitch to TV. If you have a TV personality as a host or honorary chair, work with that person to secure advance publicity with that station. You can still get great exposure without that celebrity host by doing a demonstration of what's to come at the event or offering an event site interview with a news-making civic leader who helps as a volunteer. Noon news programs love in-studio interviews with the anchorperson and the event coordinator chatting about the shindig that week and the excitement and drama you're certain to enjoy at the annual gala. To improve your chances of advance exposure, take advantage of any media connections your volunteers might have.

Support your pitching activities with a small press kit. It should contain your pitch letter, the announcement news release, a fact sheet on your organization, a backgrounder on your group, and a one-page listing of your corporate sponsors and committee chairs. This information will save a reporter time by answering most of the general or overview types of questions, such as, "How will you use the money raised at the event?" Copy and paste the information into an e-mail message if you are pitching with e-mail, labeling each section clearly so it doesn't all flow together. If you're pitching over the phone, ask if the reporter prefers e-mail, fax, regular mail, or hand delivery.

WORKING WITH CELEBRITIES

Celebrities bring bonus publicity potential. If you've secured a very well-known speaker many months before your annual fundraiser, send an announcement news release with the celebrity's photo as soon as the contract is signed. Newspapers will use it and, if your speaker is famous enough, so will TV and radio stations. This advance notice lets the celebrity's fans save the date on their calendars, while it gives you something to leverage with potential sponsors—if everybody's buzzing about it, businesses will certainly want to be part of the excitement.

Work with the speaker committee to ensure that your speaker contract details how much media access to the celebrity you need before and during the event. You want to make certain your newspaper can do a telephone interview in time for a feature running the week of the event. In addition, many media outlets will want to do interviews at the event, and you don't want the contract to prevent that. Media access shouldn't be a contract negotiation deal breaker, but you definitely want to make sure it's defined to prevent surprises or bad feelings. Finally, make sure your event press kit includes the celebrity's bio and photo.

In addition to these activities, create a shorter calendar announcement that you send to calendars once a week for four weeks until the

> ### Celebrity Involvement Adds Publicity Value
>
> Organizers of the Atlanta 2-Day Walk for Breast Cancer hoped publicity would dramatically increase walker registration, and donations, in the Walk's third year. To generate media exposure in advance of the September event, they hosted a Mother-Daughter Survivor Fashion Show and Celebration in May. They used celebrities to attract media attention, recruiting a local television anchorwoman as the emcee and the city's female mayor as a model. News releases, calendar listings, public service announcements (PSAs), and reminder media alerts generated publicity in various local newspapers, on two TV news programs, and on local radio stations. This visibility led to various speaking engagements for founder Randi Passoff, a two-time breast cancer survivor, who used the platform to encourage audiences to participate in the September fundraising walk. Because of the publicity, organizers had more walkers registered after the fashion show than they had in total the year before, leaving them with high hopes for a record-setting fundraising event.

week of the event. Convert that release into a PSA script that is sent to TV and radio public affairs directors four weeks in advance. Use the PSAs to encourage TV news departments to feature your event on any "good news" segments or nonprofit showcases that some stations include during evening news broadcasts.

GETTING THE MEDIA TO THE EVENT

Your next publicity assignment is to generate media attendance at the actual event. Get on the phone a week before the event with any media outlets you haven't spoken to already to determine their interest in covering your news. TV won't be able to answer that question so soon, so your goal with TV assignment editors is to make certain your announcement is in the daybook for the event date. If you're told that it's not, simply fax or e-mail another announcement. When calling TV, make sure you stress the on-site visuals that will make the coverage interesting. When calling radio—and most radio stations won't be able to attend the event but you'll want to try anyway—tell them who will be available on-site for interviews.

Fax or e-mail a media alert (see Chapter 5) highlighting the specifics just two days before the event. This is their event reminder. Make sure it includes the on-site contact name so they know whom to ask for when they arrive. The day of the event, call your contacts one more time to try to get a sense of who to expect. While TV news desks will find it difficult to commit to attending in any absolute way, they will usually tell you if they'll try to be there. By this point, you have probably had one or two conversations, if not interviews, with any print reporters planning to attend. Remind them that you're looking forward to seeing them; ask if a photographer is coming, too.

Have press kits on-site for reporters. They've received all the information already, but getting the information again at the event helps any who don't have the materials with them. It also gives you one more chance to gain some control by making sure they have a document with a correct description of your organization and the event's purpose. Get more control by remembering to do media interviews in front of the banner with your group's name and logo (or, in some cases, your largest sponsor's name and logo). Work on-site with your own photographer to capture a few shots of the media conducting interviews so you can use those photos illustrating your media success in your marketing newsletter or on your Web site.

FOLLOW-UP PUBLICITY

Work with your photographer to take good candid photos you can send to smaller publications immediately after the event. For publicity purposes, avoid those pictures where a group of three or four people smile awkwardly at the camera. Instead, get candid group shots, photos of the speakers or honorees receiving an award as it happens, and overview shots that capture the scene. A photographer with news or editorial experience will know what pictures to take. The more staged photos belong in your newsletter, on your Web site, and framed on the walls of the people participating or honored. Get your news shots as quickly as possible from your photographer and e-mail them to the smaller weekly papers that use submitted photos. Include captions that identify the people from left to right. A good cross section of people from different towns served by different papers will get your event exposure in more newspapers.

As soon as you know how successful your event was, regardless of how you're measuring success, send a news release announcing that success in specific terms—amount raised, number of attendees, projects completed, and so on. Use a quote from your executive director to thank the many volunteers as well as the general public for making that success possible.

SPECIAL OPPORTUNITIES PRESENTED BY CERTAIN EVENTS

Some events present other types of publicity opportunities worth exploring. A town hall meeting, for example, could be aired live on the local PBS affiliate or taped for broadcast later. It could also be taped and broadcast on the local public access cable network or on the local NPR station. Certain quirky events—those that are highly unusual, like a beach snowshoe race benefiting a charity—might have national publicity potential. The proceedings of a professional development conference, packaged and made available to those unable to attend, offer additional publicity opportunities. Regardless of the nature of your event, be open-minded about how you might use the event now and later for publicity purposes so that you get the most from your organization's hard work.

NEXT STEPS

Before moving on to the next chapter about preparing for media interviews, take time to do the following:

- Examine the publicity value of any annual event that your organization hosts.
- Begin thinking about ways to make the event more newsworthy. If it already contains newsworthy elements, how can you take better advantage of them?
- If your organization hasn't done an event, consider whether this is the year to start one. As you think about what would serve your purposes, think also about how to make sure it secures publicity.

10

HOW WILL YOU SAY IT ON YOUR WEB SITE?

AWeb site is an essential tool for even the smallest nonprofit organization. It isn't optional. It's a must-have, whether you're targeting technologically intense 20- or 30-somethings or people over 55. Increasing numbers of people of all ages are Web savvy, using it to find the simplest information—a local telephone number—to the most obscure fact—who was Lawrence Welk's accordion player? Today's consumers expect businesses of all sizes to have a Web site. Organizations without a Web presence risk giving the impression that they are temporary or unstable.

HIRE A PROFESSIONAL

does take a small amount of specialized knowledge. Some organizations have the necessary talent in-house, but most small nonprofits don't have the internal resources to create a truly professional site that supports the quality image and reputation of the organization. That's why the best

It's not enough simply to have a Web site, either. For it to help promote and publicize your organization, your site has to work hard as an integrated component of your marketing efforts. The site colors should match those of your letterhead and logo. Its personality should match that of your other marketing pieces. Is your group playful? The Web site must reflect that. Is your organization focused on a serious cause? Your site's look and tone must communicate that. Your Web site is an extension of all of your marketing endeavors, so make sure its look and feel is current and appropriate, especially if you've made any changes in your organization's direction or image.

All Web sites should make basic information easy to find. This includes text about the organization and its mission; its leadership; your IRS form 990; the annual report; a press room; specifics on whom to contact for more information by mail, phone, or e-mail; and, if appropriate, frequently asked questions. If you generate a lot of walk-in traffic, include driving and parking directions and a map. Sponsoring a conference this year? Include the brochure, a registration form, and the agenda. If you host many events, include a calendar. If you publish a print or electronic newsletter, upload all issues to the site so they're all accessible in an archive. View all of your communications materials as potential Web site content. When planning or updating your site, think of the questions you and others are asked most often and provide the answers on the site in the appropriate sections.

Include a mechanism for soliciting and capturing e-mail addresses, especially if you publish an electronic newsletter. Make certain you have a section that explains how people can make contributions—and if they can do it on your site with a credit card, even better. When appropriate, make it possible for people to make memorial contributions in a way that lets you send an acknowledgment card to the memorialized individual's family.

Other potential elements and features of your site—case studies, testimonials, or a blog—should be determined by what's appropriate for your goals and resources. Be open to as many content opportunities as possible, though, because a content-rich site is easier to find in an online search.

Whether your site is new or existing, make sure the Webmaster submits it to search engines so it can be found by journalists and your target audiences. If you don't take these extra steps to make certain the site is found when people use search engines, your site will be much harder to find.

If you already have a Web site, review it to make sure it communicates clearly and effectively. Keep in mind that it's not enough to have a site that looks good—it has to be functional, too. Is it easy to navigate? Is the most important information up front or do people have to dig for it? Are you missing any of the information listed above? Is your type too small or in a color that makes it hard to read? Is your site designed in frames that force people to scroll through one section—rather than the whole screen—to read even small amounts of type? You don't want to frustrate visitors. Proofread all of the text to make sure there are no errors. This is your image online. You want your Web site to be as professional as your organization.

YOUR ONLINE PRESS ROOM

Your Web site needs a "press room" containing news releases, tip sheets, backgrounders, fact sheets, and photos that can work in the background to make sure you don't miss opportunities you're not aware of. The press room is an essential Web site component, because it lets journalists access background information from your Web site easily, 24 hours a day. Journalists find many of their sources by conducting Internet searches for key phrases. They scoop up as much preliminary information as they can from the best sources' Web sites before following up with an interview. If they can't find useful information on your Web site, they might move onto another resource without contacting you. While it might be just as easy from your perspective to e-mail any requested information to a reporter, the journalist doesn't see it that way. A reporter will tell you that it's easier to copy and paste online than to find the right person and request information.

In addition to working with your Webmaster or tech guru about making sure your Web site can be found by search engines, make your press room truly valuable and not just a placeholder. It can make the difference between whether you do—or don't—get the media exposure your organization deserves.

Organize your online press room to make it easily accessible for the user. First, pay attention to the name of the page. Label it "Press Room," "For the Press," "For the Media," or "Media Information"—anything that shouts to reporters, "Look here!" Don't title it, "In the News," as some groups do. That title is generally used to showcase press clippings—the results of your publicity efforts.

Clearly identify the type of information you have available by using category titles. List document titles under each category. Categories can include news releases, fact sheets, backgrounders, photos, and so on. Under each category, list the document title (include the date for news releases) and link each title to the full document. The user clicks on the title and gets the release. Give journalists an opportunity to stay in touch with you by including a place where they can enter their e-mail address to be added to your media distribution list. If you will be sending a large number of news releases to a national media audience, explore new technologies such as RSS—real simple syndication—for distribution from your Web site.

When creating or updating your online press room, avoid some of the more common mistakes made by even the most sophisticated companies. These include requiring journalists to register to get access to your press materials; omitting the date of the document so the reporter or researcher doesn't know if it's new news or old news; omitting a contact name, phone number, and e-mail address for more information; and saving the document as a PDF file that cannot be copied and pasted into another file with all versions of Adobe Acrobat software.

TO BLOG OR NOT TO BLOG

Blogs—Web logs—are increasingly popular because they allow for free expression. Blogs are simple Web sites that are frequently updated with a series of short articles written in a personal voice. Blog entries generally contain facts and opinions in the same way that newspaper editorials do but are often less formal. Basic blogs can be created easily (and at no cost) in a matter of minutes with fill-in-the-blanks templates available online at sites such as http://www.blogger.com and http://www.wordpress.org. They can be linked to your Web site or reside on your Web site.

O*nline* P*ress* R*oom* P*rovides* T*imely* M*edical* U*pdates*

Months before surgery that would separate conjoined twins Ahmed and Mohamed Ibrahim at Children's Medical Center Dallas, the hospital turned to its public relations agency of record, Richards/Gravelle, to handle the communications planning and execution surrounding the surgery. The challenge was to provide timely information to reporters around the globe as efficiently as possible. The firm's plan covered each potential outcome of the surgery. In addition, the plan laid out how to keep reporters around the globe up-to-date on what would happen in the operating room. When surgery was completed, the agency created an online press room housing an extensive press kit. The press materials provided copious amounts of background information and a Q&A addressing tough questions. During the 34-hour operation, the agency posted condition reports every 3 hours on the Web site, answering reporters' questions before they were asked. The online press room was highly effective, allowing more than 11.3 million unique visitors in one month to follow the progress of the two boys.

The buzz on blogs is that they're a great way to communicate directly with your constituents and they're a good way to reach the media with your messages. What makes them good for your organization, then, might also make them bad. Their value lies in how they allow for direct conversation with others—conversation that includes feedback. That feedback can pose problems, because it can be negative, nasty, or misleading. Do you want the press to have access to such uncontrolled dialogue? You can eliminate the conversations with constituents, of course, by using software that doesn't allow others to respond, but in doing so, you're losing much of the value of a blog.

On the positive side, blogs allow organizations to link to blogs of other like-minded groups, forming a community. This lets you bring your concepts closer to the audience that's most receptive to your message, which might be good. Blogs are also great tools for building momentum leading to a conference or another type of event, to generate interest in a significant report that will soon be released, and for soliciting opinions.

One nonprofit uses a blog as its primary communications tool with members. Soldiers' Angels, a volunteer organization dedicated to supporting U.S. military personnel fighting overseas, uses its blog to coordinate the activities of the group's volunteers, who are located around the United States and Europe. The Soldiers' Blog is a sophisticated communications base with areas for specialized teams, current projects, state divisions, and more. All elements, and the thousands of volunteers assigned to each of them, use the online tool to stay in touch. In addition, the Blog highlights requests for assistance from soldiers and their families on a daily basis. For example, when the organization learned that a young soldier's pregnant wife and young child were living in a virtually unfurnished apartment with little to no food, clothing, or basic supplies, the information was posted on the Blog. Within an hour, volunteers were arranging to get the family food, a bed, other donated furniture, clothing, diapers, and more. For this group, a blog is a high-tech tool with a low-tech goal: letting soldiers and their families know that people care.

Before jumping on the bandwagon with a blog because you have a tech-savvy staffer who's enthusiastic about creating one or because you've heard that they're essential, consider your target audience. Is it comprised of people who spend a lot of time online and who read blogs? If your audience skews young and isn't poor, a blog might have potential. If your audience is older and very active, perhaps too busy to read online journals, a blog isn't an essential communications tool.

One good way to determine if a blog is wise is to survey your constituents. Ask them what they think. Do they read blogs? What do they like about them? What don't they like? Would they come to your site regularly to read yours? What information would your blog need to have for them to read it? Get some input from the people who matter most to your organization. It will help you make an informed decision. Note, too, that because the most useful blogs require at least weekly, if not daily, input, they are time consuming to maintain. Make sure you have the staff to do this.

Meditation **B**log **C**onnects **E**nthusiasts

MeditateNYC.org, a group of otherwise unrelated meditation centers collaborating to promote meditation in New York City, uses a blog to communicate with its audience—New Yorkers interested in, or just curious about, meditation. Volunteer blogmaster Dave Platter writes daily, posting news items, updates, links, and interviews. The organization measures the blog's success by unique visitors, number of visits, and length of stay. With an average of 1,700 visits per month, the MeditateNYC blog is more of a news resource than a source of the opinionated, highly personal commentary more typical of blogs. Using a blog format instead of a traditional news approach, however, allows Platter to write in the more conversational tone appropriate for the topics covered.

NEXT STEPS

Before moving on to the next chapter to learn about preparing and conducting a media interview, take time to do the following:

- If you don't have a Web site, start planning one. Hire a professional to help you.
- If your organization already has a Web site, review it to make certain it's working as hard as it could. Make sure it reflects any recent changes in your organization's direction or image.
- Create an online press room that contains all of your press materials and answers nearly any question a reporter would ask about your organization.

11

HOW WILL YOU SAY IT
IN AN INTERVIEW?

Once you've read this entire book, created a thoughtful and strategic publicity plan, and started using the tools and tactics you've learned, your organization will begin getting calls from the press. This is good news, as long as everyone in your organization knows about your media relations efforts; who is (and isn't) authorized to talk to the press; and who should receive telephone or e-mail media inquiries. This is important, so don't make any assumptions about who does and doesn't know what. Tell them about your media relations efforts and how you'd like media inquiries handled. Put the instructions in writing so people can refer back them when necessary.

This means, too, that if you haven't decided who can talk to the press, you'd better do so now. How you might handle this often depends on the size of the organization. In a small agency, the executive director or founder usually takes this duty. Sometimes the person responsible for communications, development, or marketing—or the person who wears all three hats—takes media calls. Or perhaps the three-hatted person is the interview screener who finds out what's needed, schedules the interview with the executive director, and helps the leader prepare. Your spokesperson should be well versed in the organization's entire operation and be well spoken. You'll want that person to communicate your organization's messages and helpful information to listeners, viewers, and readers in a relaxed, confident manner.

Some people are intimidated by the thought of media interviews, though. They worry about saying something that will reflect poorly on the organization or about looking as nervous as they feel. You can help them—or yourself—reduce that fear and anxiety by preparing for media interviews properly. Once you have done a few interviews for which you were well prepared, you'll see that these sessions can be easier than figuring out what to wear on a television talk show. And, as you gain more confidence with interviews, you'll become an even more effective communicator. Here's how to do that.

TALK ABOUT YOUR TALKING POINTS

You developed messages in Chapter 3 and you've used them in your media materials. You'll use them in interviews, too. Each time you schedule an interview, select the two or three messages (no more than three) that are most important to the topic being discussed. Each of these messages becomes a talking point that you'll want to expand on. (See the Message Development Worksheet in the Appendix.) To expand, move from the general—"We are well known for helping the area's children,"— to the specific—"Did you know that last year, the United Way honored us for our work to protect this county's children?" You can see how this fact, if used in an article, accomplishes your goal: to communicate that you do a lot for local children.

Identify supporting information for your talking points. This information will bring your message to life by putting it in context. It might be an anecdote from the organization's work, a personal story of your own, a testimonial, or a statistic. Personal stories are particularly powerful and credible. Write your supporting information under your talking point.

Let's use a message from Chapter 3 as an example of how this works: "Preparing a healthy meal doesn't take any more time than waiting in the drive-through line at your favorite fast food restaurant." The supporting information might be:

Recent research from the National Association of Fast Food Operators reveals that it takes an average of 10 minutes to get a fast food meal. Assuming people drive an additional 10 minutes out of their way to get to a restaurant on their way home from work, that's a total of at least 20 minutes. I can give you 4 recipes right now that take less time than that to prepare for dinner. Wouldn't you rather spend that time cooking something nutritious than waiting for a meal that's less healthy?

Another approach with that particular message might be to offer information about the average American's weight gain from fast food or the health risks linked to the unhealthy ingredients in certain fast food meals. Your choice of supporting material depends on the subject of the interview and the interests of the audience. A personal story might work, too:

> When our nutritionist told me this, I was skeptical, so I tried it myself. I was surprised to discover that, not only did I get home quicker when I didn't stop to pick up dinner first, but my husband and I each lost five pounds the first month we tried this approach. We felt so much better after eating a healthy dinner that we started walking at night. Not only has this helped us lose a little extra weight, but we sleep better now, too, because of the exercise.

Whenever possible, find out what others are saying about your topic to make sure your talking points are different from theirs and therefore more likely to be used, because they won't duplicate what the reporter has already learned. Does another organization in town deal with this issue, too? What has its spokesperson said before in interviews? When your messages are the same, reduce the chance that the message won't be attributed to you by saying it differently, in a way that's more surprising or memorable.

TAKE LARGE SOUND BITES

When your choice of words is memorable, clever, or unexpected, almost guaranteeing that it will be used, you're talking in "sound bites." A sound bite is a short, catchy snippet of speech that captures the essence of your message in a way that stands out in your audience's memory. Journalists love them. Politicians are famous for them—think of John F.

Kennedy's "Let us never negotiate out of fear, but let us never fear to negotiate." At the O.J. Simpson trial, Johnny Cochran said, "If the glove doesn't fit, you must acquit." On his deathbed, author William Saroyan said, "Everybody has got to die, but I have always believed an exception would be made in my case."

Think of some phrases you remember from past and present. They're memorable because they are surprising, funny, clever, shocking, or unlikely. As Mark Twain said, "The lack of money is the root of all evil." Like this one, good sound bites contain a play on words, often tweaking an established cliché. They use analogies that help us create a picture in our minds. Shortly after hurricane Katrina destroyed the Gulf Coast region, Biloxi, Mississippi, mayor A.J. Holloway told reporters, "This is our tsunami." When being interviewed about North Korea's announcement that it had nuclear weapons, former U.S. State Department official Richard Haass said, "We do not want Korea to become the Wal-Mart of the world."

Some people talk in sound bites all the time—it's their gift. Most of us need our clever turn of the phrase to be scripted, though. Start by studying sound bites. Watch the morning network talk shows to see what some of the guests are saying. These people are highly media trained. When they say something that catches your ear, it's not by chance. It's because the media trainers worked with them until they had a good list of sound bites and anecdotes. Write down the ones that catch your attention. Next, do an Internet search to find other well-known examples. Add them to your list. Look for language patterns and trends that will help you develop your own.

Write down what you want to say, then play with the language. Is there a way you can repeat a key word, as Kennedy did with the *fear* quote above? Another approach is to channel stand-up comedians. Spend a Friday evening watching the back-to-back comedians on Comedy Central, then ask yourself how one of those comedians would say your message. You'll surprise yourself with the effectiveness of what you create. Consult with a TV reporter from another city (so there's no conflict of interest) who can help you zero in on the best catch phrases or nuggets for sound bites. A broadcast reporter knows what to listen for in interviews and what makes a great quote.

Put the time into sound bite development, particularly when you plan to do broadcast news interviews, because quite often a memorable quote determines whether your interview makes it on the air. A local TV news report is built around a reporter's narrative and interviews with two or three people connected to the story, and each one of those interviews gets cut down to one or two sentences. Your sound bite is what will make sure your sentence gets used. You want to be certain that what you said was worth hearing.

PRINT VERSUS BROADCAST INTERVIEWS

There are significant differences between print and broadcast media interviews; understanding them can help you prepare and manage expectations about what might happen. One of the biggest differences is the knowledge the interviewer has about the subject you're talking about. A print reporter, whether it's for a newspaper, a magazine, or a Web-based or e-mailed publication, is interviewing several people on the topic. Each interview helps the journalist become more knowledgeable. If you're the first person interviewed, your conversation might be longer, because you are probably educating the reporter on the subject as well as providing your organization's views or perspectives. On the other hand, if you're the fourth or fifth person interviewed, the reporter is probably up to speed and is looking primarily for amplification on a specific concept or to uncover something that they haven't heard already.

Sometimes, different sources say the same thing, so one of the interviews doesn't make it into the article. The person left out is usually disappointed or, worse, angry. Unfortunately, this situation is not unusual. If it happens to you, don't chastise the reporter or the editor. Instead, send a gracious note saying you thought the article was well written and, while you are disappointed they were unable to use your interview, you hope they'll keep you in mind for other related articles. You'll have friends for life.

Back to the point about multiple interviews. This is another difference between print and broadcast interviews. While there are exceptions, more often than not, when you are interviewed on local radio or TV, you are usually the only source of *expert* information. In most cases, you aren't part of a panel. Local talk shows don't use a point-counterpoint approach such as national morning news programs use for controversial subjects. In addition, unlike print reporters, talk show hosts aren't expected to educate listeners and viewers on the subject—that's your job. They haven't done much homework to prepare for the interview; they're counting on you to zero in on what's relevant or important. If you've done your job well, the homework they *have* done has come from you—you've sent background information and a list of good questions to ask.

That doesn't mean you won't face an antagonistic situation, because you very well might. If your topic is controversial, that's why you're on the air—controversy sells. Be prepared for your interviewer to take the opposite stand, regardless of personal beliefs, just to generate drama. And, if the interviewer truly is on the other side of the fence, they will share their own stories to which you'll have to respond. This is far less likely to happen in a print interview.

Another difference between print and broadcast interviews is the end product. You might spend 30 minutes on the telephone with a newspaper reporter, but the resulting article only uses 1 or 2 direct quotes. This is how balanced reporting works. Don't be disappointed or infer that it means your spokesperson did a bad job. TV news interviews produce similar results—just a few sentences get used, no matter how long your interview takes. When it comes to radio and TV talk shows (versus news shows), however, everything you say goes over the airwaves. Sometimes your radio talk show interviews will be taped and shortened, but more typically you're on the air when you're talking or your interview runs exactly as taped. This holds true whether you're doing a 30-minute radio talk show program or just one segment of a local morning talk show.

Where you are interviewed differs, too. For TV, you might be interviewed at an event, a location related to the topic, at your office, or in the studio. If your newspaper article relates to an event, you could be interviewed in person on-site. More typically for newspapers, magazines, and radio, you're interviewed by phone. A phone interview has two key benefits. First, it allows you to keep your message or talking points in front of you, so you worry less about remembering what to say. Second, you don't have to worry about what to wear. In-person interviews have their benefits, though, so if given a chance to go into the radio studio to do the interview, do it. Being face-to-face can help tone things down when the subject is controversial, because it's harder to be confrontational in person. Eye contact with the interviewer helps in all situations. So does body language.

YOU'VE GOT AN INTERVIEW: NOW WHAT?

You've pitched a story, and your media contact has called for an interview. Start to prepare immediately. Preparation is essential for success, especially with people with little media interview experience. When scheduling the interview, ask the reporter a few questions that will help you prepare. Begin with: "I haven't done a lot of interviews, so do you mind if I ask a few questions that will help me make sure I give you what you're looking for?" Then ask questions from one of these lists.

For print interviews:

- What is the topic?
- What's your interview deadline?
- Who else are you interviewing?
- How much time do you need?
- Do you need additional background from us?

For broadcast interviews:

- What is the topic?
- Who will do the interview?
- Will other people be interviewed and, if so, who are they?
- Where will the interview take place?
- How long will it last?
- Do you need additional information from us?
- Is there anything else you think I should know?

If you have to schedule the interview for someone else, make sure you get to that person's calendar as quickly as possible. Even if you promise to call back with schedule options, if it takes too long to set up the interview, you could lose the opportunity.

When you don't know much about the journalist, find out as much as you can. An interview with a TV station's investigative reporter isn't the same as an interview with the health reporter. Knowing even a little bit about the journalist and the types of questions that reporter typically asks helps you anticipate what to expect.

Use mock interviews to help your spokesperson practice incorporating the talking points and to explore how to deal with more difficult or antagonistic questions. Using the knowledge gained from the questions you asked when the reporter called, put yourself in the reporter's shoes

Campaign **U**ses **Q**uotes, **I**nterviews, **E**xclusively

Grameen Foundation USA (GFUSA) uses tiny loans, financial services, and technology to help the poor in developing countries start self-sustaining businesses to escape poverty. To secure media coverage about GFUSA's mission, Wasabi Publicity, Inc. works to have GFUSA's experts and spokespeople quoted regularly by the press on relevant topics in the news. It uses a combination of methods—monitoring media inquiries through the subscription service, ProfNet, and faxing and e-mailing expert quotes on relevant current events to its media database. Reporters use the quotes in stories they're working on or interview the experts over the phone. To make certain those experts comment appropriately on the news while dispensing the organization's key messages, Wasabi provides media training. This opportunistic approach relies on well-trained, knowledgeable experts to link GFUSA to the issues it supports.

and ask questions one might logically expect for a story or report on that subject. Nearly every answer offered by your spokesperson has to include one of your talking points. Doing so takes a small amount of creativity and practice, so . . . practice, practice, practice. It can be as easy as tacking your talking point onto your answer: "That's why we always say that it takes less time to cook a nutritious meal than it does to pick up fast food."

An interviewer won't always ask the questions that will allow you to respond with your talking points, but you can overcome this challenge. You will need to transition from the question you don't want to answer to the one you do want to answer. This is known as "bridging." Politicians have mastered this skill, as you'll notice when you pay attention to their television interviews. Do they really ever answer the question? No, but you sure know where they stand on the issue they want to talk about.

You can bridge from the question asked to the answer you want to give in a number of ways. One approach is to say, "That's a good question, but the one we hear most about this subject is . . . ." Another approach is, "I don't know the answer to that question, but what I *do* know is . . . ." You can also say, "Before I answer that question, I'd like to point out that . . . ." Work on this until you feel comfortable offering those talking points as part of nearly every conceivable answer.

Role-play with off-base, peculiar, or hostile questions, too. Reporters thrive on drama and conflict, so it's important to be prepared for questions that seem antagonistic. You don't have to have the answers to all the questions, but you do have to respond appropriately. Never say, "No comment." Those two words make it look like you have something to hide, even if you don't. Better options include, "I wish I had the answer to that question," "I don't have the answer to that question," "I'm not prepared to talk about that," or, "That's beyond the expertise of my organization." On the other hand, when it's a reasonable question that you should have an answer to but don't, promise to get the information and get it to the journalist later.

The preparation for hostile questions is particularly important for spokespeople who distrust the press and for topics or situations that are already controversial. Preparation is less important when your topic is inherently less controversial, but even so, it helps to role-play with every possibility so you never feel ambushed. You are in a better position to control the interview—and your own behavior—when you are prepared for all scenarios.

HANDLING YOURSELF IN AN INTERVIEW

You're familiar with the media outlet and the journalist, you know what you want to say, and you've practiced saying it. Now you're ready to do the interview. Here are some tips to keep in mind:

- *Stand up when doing telephone interviews.* You'll be more animated and your voice will have more energy, which is particularly important for radio interviews. Make sure you do this if you're doing a pre-interview for a national TV talk show, too, because those producers are especially concerned about guests' energy level.
- *Use your host's name when doing the interview.* It's your host's favorite word.
- *Don't talk too fast.* It's hard for a radio audience to listen to and it makes it harder for a print reporter to take notes. Use a friendly, conversational tone.
- *Keep responses brief while saying what you need to say.* "Too much information" applies here, too. Avoid yes and no answers on talk

shows. If you're asked a yes/no question, answer correctly but elaborate.

- *Don't use industry jargon.* It interferes with communication when people don't understand it—and if it's jargon, they probably don't. Health care practitioners are especially guilty of this, using *scrip* instead of *prescription* and talking about *edema* when what they mean to say is that a patient's feet were swollen with retained water.
- *Don't say anything you wouldn't want to see in print or hear on the news.*
- *Never go off the record.* Speak with the understanding that what you say will be used. If you don't want to be quoted, don't say it.
- *If you make a mistake during a taped interview, ask to do it over.*
- *Correct inaccuracies or misperceptions.* But do it politely in a way that preserves the interviewer's dignity.
- *Help the interviewer understand what's most important by saying so.* Say, "The most important thing readers need to know is . . . ." Say it often if you have to.
- *When the interviewer asks if you'd like to add anything, provide additional important information or repeat your most important talking point.* "I'd just like to repeat that what's most important here is . . . ," or, "I'd like to repeat what people can do to help . . . ."

TIPS FOR TV INTERVIEWS

In television interviews, it matters what you wear. You also might be sitting in a studio and unable to give your voice energy by standing. The secret to success with TV interviews is not to get too comfortable. That sounds counterintuitive, but it's a fact. As already noted, TV cameras magically drain your energy. You have to counter that by being less relaxed and more animated. Become less comfortable by sitting straight on the edge of the chair with your hands placed loosely in your lap rather than leaning back in the chair and draping your arms over its arms. Smile. Smile even though you're uncomfortable as heck. We like looking at smiling people more than we like looking at frowning people (probably because they're uncomfortable because they're not leaning back in their chair) or those who are expressionless. Even if your topic is sad, use a slight smile so you don't make viewers uncomfortable by seeming morose.

With a smile in place, use your hands when you talk. That's why they're loose on your lap and not clasped together so tightly that your knuckles turn white. You know you talk with your hands naturally—you are probably tongue-tied if you have to sit on your hands. You want to communicate on television just as naturally as you do at work or at home—so free those hands up and use them to gesture and make a point. This will help you seem more animated because it will help you *become* more animated.

The big question for somebody being interviewed on a television talk show for the first time is "Where do I look?" You can always spot the novices when watching TV interviews—they are the ones whose eyes dart from the camera to the host and back to the camera again. The poor guest doesn't know if they should be talking to viewers directly through the camera, as a news reader does, or looking at the host. Unless instructed otherwise, always look at the host, even when you are introduced. Remember that line from the Wizard of Oz, "Pay no attention to that man behind the curtain?" The camera is the man behind the curtain. The only time you'll need to look directly into the camera is when you're doing a remote interview, which is when the host is asking you questions from the studio and you're somewhere else, or when you're taking calls from viewers.

What to Wear on TV

The next question is: What to wear, what to wear? This is important—impressions do make a difference, especially in a visual medium. People have been known to underdress and overdress. You want to wear what's appropriate for your job, if that's why you're being interviewed. If you're a zookeeper, don't wear a suit for a television appearance. Yes, it's professional, but it confuses viewers, who have never seen a zookeeper wear a suit at a zoo. If you run a playground, don't wear your best dress clothes. Wear your best playground clothes. You don't want viewers to be even momentarily distracted or confused by your apparel.

Study the show to see what the hosts and guests wear. If the host always wears a suit, and a suit is appropriate for your job, then wear a suit. At the same time, if you're a woman and the female host always wears a dress and you don't—ever—you'll need an acceptable alternative that allows you to be comfortable. It's important that you feel like yourself, and that won't happen if you feel as though you're wearing a costume. Will your favorite outfit fit in? That's the one to go with. Need an excuse to go shopping? This is the excuse you've been looking for!

Whatever you wear, keep it plain and conservative so it doesn't distract the viewer. Don't wear busy patterns such as checks, stripes, and plaids—they're hard on the eyes. Avoid wearing white, especially around the face, because of the way it reflects light. It will drain you of color (and remember, TV already drains your energy). Men should wear dark suits or jackets with blue or off-white shirts, or a solid-colored sweater or shirt when not wearing a jacket. Women should be very careful with accessories, selecting those that allow for that essential statement of personal style, but that don't overwhelm them or the outfit. You don't want people admiring your funky earrings or that fabulous scarf. You want them watching your lips, listening to your words. Women should use heavy pancake makeup, too. You might feel like a kabuki actress, but you will look natural—not washed out—on TV.

COMMUNICATING IN A CRISIS

Interviews conducted during a crisis aren't easy. Something bad has happened and nobody is happy about it, yet you have to face the press and answer questions. What you say is important, but so is how you say it. Remember that tip about smiling? It doesn't apply here. Your face should reflect the gravity of the situation. If you're tired because of the strain caused by the crisis, it's okay to show that. At the same time, you want to appear strong and confident so you inspire faith in your organization as well as your words. Most situations benefit from an attitude of compassion and confidence—compassion with the opposing view or the victims, confidence that you will do the right thing.

Every nonprofit organization should have a crisis communications plan on file. This is particularly important for organizations that are by definition embroiled in controversy—abortion clinics come to mind. But others—hospitals, political organizations, schools, churches—might also face an unexpected crisis from activists, scandals, accidents, or other tragedies or disasters. The hospital accepting patients from a serious bus accident needs to be just as prepared to get information to the press as the press officer of the married politician just caught smooching with his girlfriend in Belize.

If you don't have a crisis communications plan in place and you're facing a crisis, start by formulating a communications strategy. Begin with your goal. What do you want to achieve? And how do you want to be known when all is said and done? Then figure out how you'll get there with communications tools. Keep the organization's various audiences in mind, remembering that different audiences require different tools and tactics. In addition, establish a direct line of communication to all of these audiences, using somebody they trust to share the information.

The best rule of thumb for communicating during a crisis is this one: *share what you know when you know it.* It is the only sure way to maintain your credibility in the crisis and in the future. When faced with an adversarial situation with activists, advocates, or victims, put yourself in their shoes. Understanding their perspective will help you craft talking points that address their interests, not yours. And that is a key point. When your organization is being painted as the bad guy—whether rightly or wrongly—you are automatically in the worst position. You are guilty until proven innocent. You want to be the calm voice that empathizes with your adversaries—in fact, shows *compassion* for your adversaries—while making your point. And what is your point? That comes from your strategy. Initially, it might be, "We are disturbed by these allegations [compassion] and are investigating the situation. We will share what we learn as soon as we know more."

Regardless of the situation, you want to share what you know when you know it, because you will have more control if you are the information source. You don't want others releasing and spinning that information first, no matter what the nature of the crisis. It should come from you so it is accurate and undistorted. If your organization has a blog, use it to communicate important information so those following the situation will get that information from you quickly.

To make sure there are no internal information leaks, make it clear to all employees that all communication must come only from designated spokespeople. They also need to understand that what they say about the situation outside work can have serious, negative ramifications, too. Help them understand how harmful casual comments can be to the organization, because comments to a friend can find their way to a reporter. Make it clear that leaks often contain misinformation and can confuse or worsen the situation, so they can't be tolerated.

> ### Society Uses Crisis to Create Goodwill
>
> The Fortune Society in New York City has been aiding ex-offenders with issues surrounding reentry into society since 1967. It accepts everyone, regardless of the crime. One of those criminals in 2004 was perhaps the most notorious in recent history, child-killer Joel Steinberg. While the massive media attention surrounding Steinberg's case exposed the Society to criticism and scorn, the organization remained true to its mission. To counter the negative attention, it worked with Morris, King, and Company to showcase its work in a positive way and raise awareness of the issues associated with ex-prisoner reentry. The executive director became the sole spokesperson, using scripted messages and talking points in interviews and never discussing Steinberg's situation, addressing only the organization's services. The Society also maintained its open door policy for the media and the community, keeping lines of communication open. The careful, strategic communication allowed The Fortune Society to emerge from the process unscathed and, in fact, much better known for its good work.

Make sure your response to the crisis includes information gathering on your part among those who might have answers you don't have. Your good relationships within the community will come in handy now. Find out what others know, what they don't know, and what people are saying by asking those questions of key outside contacts. Gather as much "intelligence" as you can so you're not operating in a vacuum.

For those who think, "It can't happen here," and have no intention of creating a general crisis communications plan, here are a few examples of the kinds of crises you might encounter and messages that might address them.

- Your organization is one of the best known in the community, and your executive director, a local celebrity, dies suddenly and unexpectedly at the age of 42. You want to express your genuine sadness while reassuring constituents that your organization will survive this tragedy. Message:

    We are shocked and stunned. Our thoughts and prayers are with Bob's family and with our colleagues as well. We will miss him terribly, but we know how committed he was to our mission. Now, more than ever, we dedicate ourselves to achieving the goals that were so important to him.

- The bookkeeper was arrested for embezzling funds. You are concerned that programming will suffer from the loss of funds already received and that future contributions will be negatively impacted. Message:

  > We have cooperated fully with the authorities during this investigation. We have already taken steps to ensure this can't happen again. We are still assessing the impact of this activity on our programs and will share what we learn as soon as we know more.

- Your human resources director was arrested in a prostitution raid. You want to make it clear that in this case, what Mike does in his free time has no impact on your organization. Message:

  > Mike has always done a wonderful job for us and I'm sure he'll continue to do so.

- Your human resources director was arrested in a prostitution raid, and your organization's mission is to get prostitutes off the street. (It is clear that Mike was acting as a customer that night, not a social worker.) You want to acknowledge that this is an odd development yet show compassion for your colleague. Message:

  > Mike has always done a wonderful job for us, but I'd be lying if I didn't say I'm surprised by this development. I'll be in a better position to comment after I talk to Mike.

MEDIA TRAINING

Everybody who is terrified of media interviews or expects to be doing media interviews on a continual basis should consider professional media training. A good media trainer can help you make your messages media friendly, identify the best anecdotes to go with your talking points, and handle an impromptu stand-up television interview without looking like a deer caught in the headlights. You'll get advice on how to present yourself on camera, handle difficult questions, be confident instead of defensive in challenging media situations, and maintain your composure. You'll be videotaped in role-playing situations so that you can see for yourself where you shine and where there's room for improvement.

The best media trainers are television journalists. Look for one who is no longer working for a local station so that you avoid any conflict of interest—or hire one from another city. You can also ask local public relations practitioners whom they might recommend, check your phone book, or type *"media training"* and your city into a search engine to see what comes up. When hiring a trainer, be specific about why you need the training so that the trainer focuses on only the services that are necessary.

NEXT STEPS

Before moving on to the next chapter to learn when and how to plan a press conference, take time to do the following:

- Inform staff of the company's publicity efforts and who should receive all media inquiries.
- Gather the supporting information for your messages and talking points. Collect anecdotes from colleagues. Ask the executive director to begin thinking about their own personal stories. Conduct the research necessary to gather the statistics you might need.
- Study your media outlets to determine what appeals to the media gatekeepers. What gets quoted in print articles? What are people interviewed on broadcast news or talk shows saying? What makes their choice of words memorable?
- Begin looking for sample sound bites you can deconstruct. Do an Internet search to find famous sound bites that have withstood time, but watch TV talk shows to see how highly trained spokespeople chose their words. What catches your attention? What makes you think, "That was clever"?

12

HOW WILL YOU SHARE YOUR MESSAGE AT A PRESS CONFERENCE?

A press conference allows an organization to make a major announcement of something important to the media. To underscore the significance of the announcement, a press conference is usually hosted by the head of the organization. This person presents the news, and then answers reporters' questions. A press conference is often the most effective and efficient way to make a major news announcement or respond to a crisis.

At the same time, press conferences are risky, because it's hard to get reporters to attend if you aren't announcing something the media gatekeepers believe their audiences want to read or hear. Unless you're in a small market and past experience tells you that reporters will attend, move toward a press conference with caution. You don't want your management to be disappointed or worse, embarrassed.

Ironically, the factor that makes a press conference the most appealing—gathering all local news media outlets in one place to receive the same news at the same time—is what makes it the riskiest option for getting your news out. Call a few veteran publicists and ask them to talk about their experiences with press conferences. Most will have at least one or two instances where the media was diverted by breaking "hard" news. The leaders of a technical school, for example, were disappointed when the ribbon cutting for a new building was preempted by a crash involving a school bus. Nearly every reporter who planned to attend the ribbon-cutting/press conference had to rush to the accident instead. It doesn't happen all the time, but you have to take into account this risk when planning your press conference. Also, the media may not attend for other reasons.

Because you've learned in earlier chapters about the importance of studying the media outlets you're targeting, you have probably seen a representative sampling of press conferences on the local evening news. They have most likely been hosted by the mayor, a prominent county official, a visiting statewide elected official, the CEO of the area's largest employer, and, well, you get the picture. Most local press conferences are hosted by people who make news no matter what's going on. Reporters flock to events involving these individuals because they're considered newsworthy wherever they go. If the head of your organization is a widely sought out, respected celebrity, somebody who runs in the same circles as the most prominent elected officials and corporate leaders, you have an advantage. Even so, you need news for a press conference. Here are some guidelines to help you decide when you should and shouldn't use this tactic.

WHEN TO HOLD A PRESS CONFERENCE

The worst reason to hold a press conference is because somebody else thinks it's a good idea. Press conferences are misunderstood by those who don't work with the media on a regular basis. The average business person doesn't realize how much competition there is for the media's time. A lot is going on in your community on any given day, and getting the press to cover your story instead of somebody else's can be a challenge. Getting them to show up at a specific time—especially when something more newsworthy is going on—makes it even harder. On the other hand, a press conference is a great idea in some situations, especially when you plan to have a built-in audience, making it less obvious if reporters don't show up (more about that later).

Here are just a few situations where a press conference makes sense in the right market. As you probably already know, it's a lot harder to get the media to attend a press conference in a big city like New York, Chicago, or Los Angeles than it is in a smaller city.

- You're launching a capital campaign by announcing a very, very large donation. This works best if the benefactor will attend and speak.
- You have hired an executive director with a national reputation outside your field—for example, the former president of Harvard or the retired CEO of a Fortune 100 corporation—and that person attends the press conference to speak and answer questions.
- You are launching a far-reaching, widespread consumer education campaign that will be impossible for most area residents to overlook.
- The celebrity spokesperson for your national parent organization is visiting your facility.
- You have bad news and want to present the facts before rumors start.
- Your arts organization is announcing the season's concert, performance, or exhibit schedule and the lineup includes blockbuster names.
- You are introducing the first anything in the country.
- Your organization is large and prominent and is merging with another local nonprofit that is also well known.
- Your organization is the United Way (or your community's equivalent), and you're announcing the annual campaign, its goals, and what makes this campaign different from past years' efforts. Similarly, you'll want to host a press conference to announce campaign results.
- You're announcing significant research findings that support the public policy changes favored or supported by your organization.
- You're announcing plans and new twists for a well-known annual fundraising event, such as a biking event that takes over city streets or a dinner that always features a national celebrity.
- You have controversial or timely facts and information that could influence a pending vote or decision.

All of these concepts have something in common: they're announcing news (good or bad) that the community wants to hear. Important news, as already noted, is no guarantee that you'll get the coverage you seek. But if you don't have news, you can be certain you won't get the attention of the press.

GUARANTEED ATTENDANCE

The best way to guarantee you'll have bodies in the seats at your press conference is to fill those seats with people who are interested in your announcement but aren't reporters. That way, your leader makes the announcement to people who are truly interested, even if reporters get pulled away by more dramatic, timely news elsewhere. Your spokesperson also has a much larger audience to address, because most communities don't have enough media outlets to generate more than a handful of attendees at a press conference, even with maximum media turnout.

Gather a larger audience by treating the announcement less like a press conference and more like a celebration or a rally, depending on the situation. Send appropriate invitations to members of the board of directors, elected officials, corporate leaders, individuals served by your organization, employees with a connection to the announcement, vendors, volunteers, activists, and so on. Invite these people by explaining that the organization is making an announcement they'll want to hear. Avoid using the phrase *press conference* with this audience, because that could confuse or mislead them. Include refreshments and space to network and mingle. Hire a photographer to take photos before, during, and after the announcement; the presence of a camera will make it seem as though you have media coverage even if you don't. The expense of a photographer won't be wasted—you can use the photos in your newsletter, on your Web site, and as gifts for attendees.

Press conference location affects attendance, too. Host your event at a central location that is convenient to the press and has good parking. If key media outlets are located downtown and your facility is 20 minutes away, rent a downtown location for the occasion. (The exception to this guideline is when your facility is part of the announcement for one reason or another.) Easy parking is essential for your non-media guests, as well, so make that a priority. Some announcements benefit from an offbeat or unexpected location. For example, the capital campaign announcement could happen at the site of a building that will be constructed with campaign funds, or the opera series announcement might take place in a theater. Be imaginative, be creative, but also be practical and realistic. If it's hard for people to get to your venue, there's a good chance they won't bother.

Press **C**onference **H**elps **E**nvironmental **C**ampaign

When the California Coastal Conservancy was debating whether to purchase Ormond Beach in southern California, local environmental activists were anxious. If the Conservancy didn't buy the wetlands, an oil company would buy the site for a liquefied natural gas terminal. Activists were concerned about the risk of an environmental disaster. To encourage the Conservancy to purchase the land, they retained the services of Fenton Communications, a public interest communications firm, to showcase public support for saving the wetlands. Among other tactics, such as local radio ads, the firm coordinated a combined rally and press conference at Ormond Beach a week before the Conservancy vote. More than 100 activists waved signs during presentations from speakers—elected officials, a Native American leader, and actor Beau Bridges—who urged the Conservancy to save the wetlands. Shortly thereafter, the Coastal Conservancy board voted to purchase the land. Conservancy staffers acknowledged that the event, ads, and media coverage played a role in the board's decision.

PRESS CONFERENCE TIMING

It's important to be strategic with the timing of your press conference, both in terms of the date selected and the time of day. As for the date, do your homework to see what else is scheduled for that day so you minimize potential conflicts. Check local Web calendar listings (most daily newspapers offer some type of schedule of events); the convention and visitors' bureau, and the places where press conferences are often held, such as hotels. You want to avoid going up against another scheduled event that is likely to be a big media draw. If people are murmuring that a local politician will announce his senatorial candidacy on a certain date, pick another one. Don't hold your press conference the day the circus comes to town and parades the animals down Main Street. The goal is to avoid any conflict that will cause people to ask, "What were you thinking?"

The best time of day is what's most convenient for the media, not your organization. For the media, that's usually midmorning and midweek—Tuesday, Wednesday, and Thursday. Don't schedule your announcement for late afternoon if you want TV coverage. By that time of day, TV news departments are busy preparing the evening newscasts. On the other hand, if you feel compelled to make an announcement but don't want it to get picked up by the press, turn it into a cocktail party announcement or announce it on a weekend or a holiday, when media staffing is reduced.

Time of day influences the refreshments you will serve, and you *will* serve refreshments. Some reporters spend their days going from scene to scene with barely enough time to grab a bite to eat, so they appreciate the nourishment. And it's plain good manners to feed your guests. The food you offer will depend on the time of day. Breakfast pastries, coffee, and tea are good for a midmorning announcement, while finger sandwiches or brownies and cookies with coffee, tea, and soft drinks make a good choice for mid-afternoon. If for some reason you need to plan your announcement for 8:00 AM or noon, then offer a breakfast or lunch buffet. People expect a meal when an event takes place at mealtime. Don't disappoint them.

ESSENTIAL PRESS CONFERENCE ELEMENTS

You've got a big announcement to make, a good date on the calendar, and a great location. What more do you need? The fun has only just begun. Now's the time to pull out a clipboard and start making a list of the basic press conference elements so you're certain you won't forget a thing. Like other kinds of special events, press conferences are very detail oriented. Without a good checklist, like the one on page 158 and in the Appendix, you might forget something pivotal. While press conference elements vary depending on the nature of the announcements, the basics are always the following:

- Big news
- Invitation list
- The media invitation
- A non-media invitation for other guests

- A convenient location that can handle your press conference needs—size of group, food and beverage requirements, audiovisual equipment, and so forth
- At least one speaker who makes the announcement (sometimes more)
- A news release or press kit
- Signage with your organization's name and logo
- Seating for guests
- Seating for speakers
- Follow-up phone calls
- Plenty of on-site staffing

News. Begin planning by identifying the news you will be announcing. This will determine the tone or personality of your press conference. Some situations benefit from props or decorations that help create a festive environment, while others don't. Begin thinking about press conference visuals—poster-size photographs, for example—that could provide an interesting backdrop for the announcement or give TV cameras something to videotape besides the speaker. Will there be a demonstration? You'll need room for that.

Invitation list. Who should be on your invitation list? Don't invite every media contact in your database unless this is the type of story they cover. Just because the sports reporter covered your 10K fundraiser doesn't mean they should (or would) attend the announcement about your exciting new consumer education campaign. Their colleague from the metro desk or living section would be a better choice. And, if you're venturing into new territory with this announcement and aren't sure who to invite, do your homework now to get those answers. You don't want to throw the invitation out there and see who comes. You want a thoughtful, organized approach, inviting only those who are likely to attend. You'll have to follow up each invitation with a call to see who is attending, so don't make any more work for yourself than you have to.

Invitations. Use different invitations for the media and non-media guests. You don't need a fancy, elaborate, or impressive invitation for the press. They just need to know the basics in a media alert (see Chapter 5)—who, what, when, where, and why. In fact, a traditional event invitation might be confused with a personal invitation and not get the attention it deserves. Fax the media alert that tells them what's happening and why they need to be there. How much do you tell them? That depends on the announcement, but in general, you need to give them enough information to make a decision about attending without telling them so much that they don't need to attend. A more traditional invitation is appropriate for other invitees.

Location. Make sure the location meets the criteria for accessibility. Visit the function room you'll be using to determine where to put the speakers. Will they need to speak from a platform with a lectern so they're visible? Chairs for guests will be in front of the speakers. Where will the food be? You'll need quiet space away from the hubbub for private one-on-one interviews after the announcement—is there room for that? What about audiovisual equipment? Will you need a microphone, a television, a projector for a PowerPoint presentation? Most hotel sales people will have a good checklist for you to work from, but create your own as well so nothing is left out.

Speaker. The speaker is typically the leader of the organization, who sometimes is joined by a colleague or someone else with specialized knowledge who might elaborate on specific details or answer questions. Keep it to one or two speakers who truly have something to say. Nothing is worse at any kind of event—let alone a press conference—than having to sit through speakers who are in front of the microphone for political reasons, not because they have anything substantive to contribute. Keep the combined length of all remarks to less than ten minutes. Remember: This is a news announcement, not a lecture.

Script. Script your speakers. They need to know ahead of time what they'll say and how to say it—and so will you. Remember to allow enough time in the planning process to write and rehearse their remarks. Each speaker needs to say something distinctly different from the other so there is no overlap; at the same time, they must communicate the same message. Make sure your messages and talking points are incorporated into their remarks. Give their scripts simple, powerful language. While some people prefer to talk without a script—and that is actually the best way to make a presentation—you need to be certain your speakers are experienced enough to use your carefully constructed messages or talking points without having them scripted.

Role-play. Role-play possible questions and answers. Help your speakers develop 30-second answers for radio and TV reporters. Work on sound bites to make them more quotable with all reporters. During the role-playing, ask questions that seem to be off-topic, too. It's not uncommon for a reporter to use time with a local personality, especially an elected official, to try to get a quote or comment for another news story. Your speaker needs to know how to deflect that—"Let's talk about that later, Jason."—and stay on point. There should be no surprise questions for press conference speakers. Preparation and practice are both essential.

Schedule the time. Schedule your speakers' time on-site so that it allows for one-on-one interviews after the main announcement. Reporters like to ask questions nobody else has offered publicly—it helps differentiate their story—in a private interview. If a newspaper reporter wants an in-depth interview for a long article, do the TV and radio interviews first so they don't have to wait around (and they probably won't anyway).

Press kit. Prepare a press kit to distribute to reporters as they arrive. Giving it to them when they come in allows them to read through it in time to generate informed questions. It also helps them see if any essential information is missing, so they can get it before they leave. Don't worry about reporters bolting as soon as they get the press kit so they can file a story before anyone else does. Good reporters don't want to work off just a news release; they want to ask questions and, with TV news, get good visuals to go with the story. They can't do that with a press kit alone.

The announcement press kit should contain as much or as little as needed for anybody to report the story. At a minimum, you'll need an announcement news release that has all the relevant facts and details. Depending on the story, you might need to include a backgrounder or two, a fact sheet, and a photo. The press kit distributed when a nonprofit organization announced that Maya Angelou would speak at its fundraising dinner included an announcement with the event details— date, time, place, and so on—a brief biography on Angelou, a backgrounder describing the organization and its work, and a photo of Angelou. These materials were used again closer to the event date. Don't include promotional materials such as posters, ad slicks, or brochures in the press kit unless they're part of the news, as they might be when announcing a public education campaign.

Signage. Signage at the press conference helps reinforce your organization's identity in the minds of attendees and people who might see it in a newspaper photo the next day or on a TV newscast. It's part of the brand-building process. When watching news reports that evening, your executive director would rather see the organization's logo on the podium than the Hilton logo, so make sure you order a podium sign. Hang a banner with your name and logo behind the speakers as a backdrop. Got buttons with a campaign theme? Wear 'em. TV cameras zoom in on such random visuals during otherwise fairly static events. It's important always to be thinking about what the TV cameras need to capture and to give them as much visual variety as possible.

Seating. Don't make the mistake of having too much seating. While you want to be able to accommodate the crowd, having too many empty chairs looks like you gave a party and nobody came. Be flexible on the seating instructions given to the staff at the press conference site until you have a head count you believe you can rely on. Protect the first row or two, depending on how many you're expecting, by putting "reserved for press and speakers" signs on them. If your speakers will be sitting on a dais, then make sure enough chairs are up there for them. Then put out fewer chairs than you need for other guests, forcing a standing-room-only situation. Have event staffers prepared to bring in more chairs quickly if necessary, but think twice about whether you want to. Nothing says "success" better than having a few sturdy souls standing in the back while most other seats are filled.

Follow-up. Even though your invitations included RSVP information, you will have to make follow-up phone calls to the media. Invite the press two weeks in advance, send a follow-up reminder invitation a week before, send a third reminder two days before, and call the day before to remind yet again. Do not send reminders to anyone who has RSVPed. It is acceptable to call those who have RSVPed the day before just to remind them nicely that you're looking forward to seeing them at the press conference.

Staff the event. Staff accordingly so that one person isn't responsible for everything. You'd rather have too many than too few helpers. Bring in your most responsible people, even if this isn't exactly in their job descriptions. Areas of responsibility should include the following:

- *Speaker management.* Does your speaker have their speech? (If not, the person with this job has a back-up hard copy.) Is the computer connected properly to the projector? Is the microphone working? Are there enough chairs on the dais for the person making introductions and for the speakers?
- *Food and beverage.* Did the facility provide what you ordered? Is there enough? Keep an eye on the coffee because it goes low first. Are there hot water and tea bags?
- *Sign-in.* Ask reporters and guests to sign in with their name, e-mail address, and phone number.
- *Press kits.* Press kits are reserved for the media only (others will not necessarily understand this). You can place them under the "Reserved for the Media" signs on the front seats, or you can assign the person handling guest registration to pass them out individually when reporters arrive.
- *The timer.* This is a good job for the organizer. It is the timer's responsibility to get people into place for the formal presentation so you stay on schedule.
- *People herders.* When your press conference doubles as a celebration, you might need to encourage people to take their seats at the appropriate time.

Remember that, with so many staffers helping, a reporter might ask questions of someone other than your spokesperson. Brief staff to defer all questions related to the announcement or organization to the spokesperson.

Immediately after the press conference ends, fax the announcement news release to media outlets that didn't attend.

Press Conference Checklist

Beforehand . . .

Event planning

_____ Select appropriate date, time, place

_____ Reserve best location for event size, personality, and budget

_____ Select speakers

_____ Develop invitation lists—media and others

_____ Create and mail invitations

_____ Arrange for food and beverages

_____ Write script

_____ Hire photographer

_____ Assign on-site responsibilities to staff

_____ Rehearse speakers

_____ Make follow-up calls to invitees who have not responded

_____ Send reminder media alert to press

_____ Create event timetable

_____ Create staff list that outlines responsibilities

_____ Arrange for on-site AV equipment, telephones, and specific technical capabilities if needed

_____ Discuss room set-up with facility

_____ Create press materials

_____ Create checklist of RSVP'd guests for use on-site

Invitations—include:

_____ Date and start time with brief agenda

_____ Street location of venue and parking information if necessary

_____ Brief description of press conference purpose

_____ Names and titles of speakers

_____ RSVP name, phone number/e-mail, and deadline

_____ Indication of food and beverages offered (coffee and snacks, cocktails, breakfast buffet, etc.)

On-Site

Room set-up

_____ Electrical outlets—are they where you need them to be?

_____ Light switches for room darkening if required for presentation

_____ AV equipment: Is it what you need? Does it work?

_____ Telephones

_____ Food and beverage set-up

____ Registration desk

____ Nametags (if used)

____ Signage

____ Chairs

____ Coat check

____ Name cards for speakers (if on a panel)

____ Display materials, including products

____ Raised platform for speakers

____ Press materials

____ RSVP checklist at registration table

____ Pens and pads of paper at registration table

Speaker set-up

____ Table

____ Chairs

____ Podium

____ Props

____ Name cards for speakers (if on a panel)

____ Script

____ Microphone

____ AV materials (PowerPoint presentation? Flip chart? Poster board?)

OTHER PRESS CONFERENCE OPTIONS

National organizations are increasingly turning to virtual press conferences—those conducted over the Internet through Webcasting or through telephone conference calls—to reach a large audience with their news. This type of press conference is appropriate when the media outlets interested in your message are far flung. Internet-based press conferences involve a live event that is broadcast online. Participants watch Webcasts in real time, queuing up to ask questions. Teleconferences—those taking place over the telephone without cameras—may have a Web component through an online PowerPoint presentation that accompanies spoken comments.

For both types, sophisticated technology tells you who is participating; later, it can tell you not only who was there but when and for how long. And because you know who's online—or on the phone line for teleconferences—you can instruct the operator to take calls from your "high priority" reporters first. Webcasts can also be made available on your Web site later, in edited or unedited form.

NEXT STEPS

Before moving on to the next chapter about writing your publicity blueprint, a publicity plan, take time to do the following:

- Determine if a press conference is the smartest option for your big news announcement.
- Brainstorm how to turn this event into more than a press conference, so that you don't rely on just the media for attendance.
- Review the press conference planning checklist on page 158 and in the Appendix to get a sense of the work involved.
- Begin thinking about the biggest pieces first—who will speak, where you'll stage the event, how you'll maximize turnout—before taking on the smaller details.
- Consider who will help out on-site so that the responsibility for different elements is shared. This preparation ensures a smoother event.

Part Four

THE PLAN

13

HOW WILL YOU BRING THIS TOGETHER? WRITING A PUBLICITY PLAN

Now that you've learned more about the tools and tactics used to generate publicity, you'll want to apply them to your organization's communications needs. This is where you blend what you learned in Part One about goals, audiences, the importance of understanding what's newsworthy, and message development with the tools and tactics you're learned in Parts Two and Three. It's where you combine all the Next Steps from each chapter into a document that shapes the action you'll take.

Because your publicity plan is your organization's blueprint for action, it's wise to use a format that works for your organization, whether that's bullet points, an outline with Roman numerals, or extended prose. The format you use isn't important. What *is* important, though, is that you put on paper what you want to do, why, how much it will cost, and who will do what and when. Assigning accountability as well as deadlines can make the difference between a publicity plan that soars and one that fizzles. (Chapter 14 provides information on skills needed for execution and advice on hiring an outside consultant.)

Here's how to pull all of your notes and ideas together into the plan first described in Chapter 1. So that you don't have to keep flipping back to Chapter 1, some of the basic information presented there is

***K**ids **C**an **M**ake a **D**ifference*

The Greater Boston Food Bank understands the power of the fundraising efforts of kids. In 1996, Dan and Betsy Nally, then nine and six years old, walked into The Food Bank days before Thanksgiving to drop off 36 turkeys they had collected from neighbors after hearing on the news about a shortage of turkeys. The Nallys have continued their effort each year since then by founding Turkeys 4 America, so far providing more than one million servings of Thanksgiving turkey to needy families. Through the public relations support of The Greater Boston Food Bank, which has included using press releases, phone and e-mail pitches, and B-roll video footage, both organizations have received national media coverage. This has included appearances on *Oprah, The Today Show,* and CNN and a feature in *People* magazine. In 2004, Turkeys 4 America went national with the help of corporate sponsors Perdue Farms and Thrivent Financial for Lutherans. The group expanded its media exposure through well publicized pre-Thanksgiving events in Boston, Chicago, and Cleveland.

repeated here. When you're done with this chapter, you will have a plan you can use to begin making things happen. Keep in mind that you might decide to create multiple publicity plans—one for the organization and one for each program or initiative. Do what works best for your work style and needs.

This chapter uses a fictitious organization—Through the Ages—and its publicity situation as a plan example. The situation is one that might apply to many organizations. The organization wants to publicize a fundraising dinner with a famous guest speaker. As this chapter unfolds, you'll see one way to write the publicity program for this event. Let it get you thinking about how you would handle this publicity situation and how you would write the publicity plan.

WHAT'S YOUR SITUATION/OVERVIEW?

For your organization's plan, review what you wrote earlier about your organization's situation/overview and make any changes, keeping in mind that you're summarizing your organization's communications situation in one or two short paragraphs. What is happening with the organization that makes publicity a priority? Are you launching a new initiative? Have you determined that the community doesn't understand the cause you represent? Are you hoping to increase awareness of your group to pave the way for an upcoming fundraising campaign? Do you need the power of the press behind you as you advocate for change?

This is not the place to recall the organization's history, to regurgitate your mission statement, or to describe what the agency does on a daily basis. Instead, this is where you articulate what's going on with your organization and why you need publicity.

Type Situation/Overview at the top of your page and tell us what it is. Here's our example.

Through the Ages Situation/Overview

Through the Ages helps people 65 and older deal with the challenges that come with aging. While several of our programs are grant-funded, we rely heavily on an annual fundraising dinner that always features a well-known celebrity speaker who can provide an inspirational message about aging. The speaker's fame allows us to attract corporate sponsors. Their contributions cover all event costs, including the speaker's high fee. As a result, the money we make on ticket sales is our event profit. Our goal this year is to increase ticket sales from 400 last year to 500 while keeping the ticket price the same. We need more exposure to sell more tickets, so we plan to generate more publicity than in the past. This year's speaker for the October 14 event is former President George Herbert Walker Bush. Our publicity plan will be executed in collaboration with the marketing committee's plan. The marketing committee is responsible for non-media relations promotional activities such as direct mail and advertising.

> **T**own **M**eetings **H**elp **H**ealth **I**nitiative
>
> After a national ranking report revealed that the health of Oklahomans is poor compared with residents of other states, community leaders in Central Oklahoma formed Central Oklahoma Turning Point (COTP) to do something about it. COTP was created to examine the area's health problems, prioritize them, and create an action plan. Leaders wanted to give citizens an opportunity to express their views and ideas, so Anglin Public Relations planned 22 town hall meetings in the Oklahoma City area. The firm scheduled the meetings where groups already gathered—professional and civic associations, neighborhood meetings, assistance programs, and even the county jail. Some 500 citizens attended the meetings, discussed the issues, completed a written survey, and signed up to receive updates and information. Their input was extremely valuable in helping COTP leaders understand the community's health priorities before creating recommendations.

WHO ARE YOUR TARGET AUDIENCES?

For your plan, review your target audience/stakeholder list. Is it still the same? Your target audiences might include the general public, a certain demographic or income level, current donors, potential donors, individuals who benefit from your services, local employers, your own employees, the board of directors, and so on. Prioritize your list of audiences, starting with the most important and working your way down. You read about who watches television news, listens to the radio, reads a newspaper, and so on. Has what you learned changed the media outlets you'll be targeting to reach these audiences? Here's that section from our fictional plan.

Through the Ages Target Audiences

- People who have attended past fundraising dinners
- Past and present individual donors
- People who have used our services for their parents or loved ones
- Republicans
- Men and women aged 50+

WHAT'S YOUR STRATEGY?

Based on what you have learned in this book, is your initial strategy for getting publicity still the best one? Your publicity plan strategy will reflect your big picture thinking and set the stage for your selection of tactics. Your strategy is essentially a summary of the direction you're going in one or two sentences. It might be to involve members of the local media in as many of your programs as possible or to develop good relationships with the two or three reporters you think will help your organization the most in the long run. It could be to leverage the information resources offered by your national parent organization to generate local media exposure, or it might be to create a communications committee that will be responsible for guiding or implementing your publicity efforts. Your strategy is the overarching thinking that sets you on the right path.

Through the Ages Strategy

- To take advantage of former President Bush's enormous popularity with the area's predominantly Republican population
- To generate publicity outside the newspaper Living section by using former President Bush's willingness to discuss his views on world events with local newspapers

---

DEFINE YOUR GOALS

How do your goals look to you now? Do they make sense? Are they relevant? A goal is a broad statement of direction that is determined by your needs. With good goals in place, you can look at each publicity tactic and ask, "Does this step help me achieve my goals?" If the answer isn't yes, the tactic should be removed from the plan. Goals are well defined but not specific or measurable. They tell you which direction you want to go, while your subsequent objectives will tell you how to get there.

Through the Ages Goals

- To generate increased attendance at the fundraising dinner
- To secure more publicity than in the past

OBJECTIVES SUPPORT GOALS

With your goals in place, you can work on objectives. Objectives are measurable targets set within a specific time frame. Objectives grow from goals and tactics to help determine your progress. Put in different terms, goals tell you where you want to go; objectives tell you how to get there—and when. Publicity objectives must be stated in very specific terms to be meaningful and useful.

Objectives are detailed, outlining the following in bulleted format:

- The expected accomplishment
- Who will do the work to make sure you succeed
- When the accomplishment will be finished
- How you will know the accomplishment has been achieved

To establish your plan's objectives, review your goals and tactics, then ask, "How will I make this happen?" Using measurable words allows you to monitor the progress of your activities as you work to achieve your goals. Adding deadlines helps you prioritize this work with your other responsibilities.

Through the Ages Objectives

- Use the speaker's high-profile status to generate buzz in newspapers, magazines, and on radio and TV news once the speaker is confirmed.
- Generate at least one newspaper major article outside the feature section that supports ticket sales before the event.
- Secure a media sponsor for each of the three key local media categories—print, radio, and television.
- Collaborate with local Republican Party leaders to reach each registered Republican Party member with information about the dinner at least twice.
- Make sure all on-site media coverage mentions our organization's name at least once.
- Have publicity in the daily newspaper promoting the event—even if just a calendar item—once a week for three weeks prior to the event.
- Have PSAs run regularly for the two weeks before the event.
- For the first time in the event's history, get TV news coverage of a speaker's appearance the week before the event, not just the night of the event.

TACTICS ARE WHAT YOU'LL ACT ON

You've been keeping track of the tactics that fit your situation as you've read the book. Tactics are what you'll do or the tools you'll employ to get publicity. They're press releases, tip sheets, op-eds, press conferences, newsworthy surveys, and so on. Tactics are the tangibles. And the tactics you select are those that will help you achieve your goals. To select the right tactics, go back to your goals and ask yourself, "What do I need to do to make this happen?" Review your current wish list of tactical options and select those that meet your needs and your budget. If you have to cut back, hang onto those tactics that will take you the farthest for the least amount of money.

Through the Ages Tactics

- Before the speaker contract is signed, make sure it specifies that President Bush will be available for media interviews before the event by telephone and at the event in person.
- Work with the event committee to make sure a quiet room is available near the function room where the press can interview President Bush before the dinner.
- Update the media list by April 14 (six months before event).
- Write a news release for all local media announcing President Bush as speaker as soon as his contract is signed with a target distribution date of April 14. Get release approved for April 14 distribution.
- At April board meeting, recruit a publicity committee chair. Have committee in place by May 14 (five months before event).
- By June 1 (four-and-a-half months before event), poll publicity committee members for relationships with journalists. Add these notes to media database.
- By June 15 (four months before event), recruit best-known anchorperson from the local TV station who is the strongest with target age group to serve as event emcee.
- Ongoing: Work closely with sponsorship committee to make sure media sponsors represent print, radio, and television. Negotiate in-kind trade—ads for sponsor identification. Provide information for ads by publication deadlines (to be determined).

Through the Ages Tactics *continued*

- Write PSA scripts promoting fundraising dinner. Distribute September 14 (one month before event).
- Write second announcement release for distribution September 14 (one month before event).
- By September 14 (one month before event), speak with President Bush's representative to outline media relations plans for the President's appearance. Provide information about your organization so he can put his interviews in context.
- On September 21 (three weeks before event), pitch daily newspaper Living section on article about elder abuse; ask reporter to include sidebar about the upcoming dinner that will help fund an elder abuse prevention program.
- On September 28 (two weeks before event), pitch daily newspaper Local section on a telephone interview with President Bush for an article to run the week before the event.
- By October 1, write any remaining press kit elements for use in advance or on-site. Elements should include announcement release, backgrounder on Through the Ages, brief bio on the president, fact sheet listing Through the Ages programs, and fact sheet listing names and titles of spokespersons who are likely to be interviewed on-site (executive director, president of board of directors, fundraiser committee chairperson, etc.)
- On October 6 (one week before event), write and fax reminder media alert.
- By October 6, write fact sheet listing special security precautions required for the former president's visit.
- On October 7 (one week before event), use your fact sheet to pitch TV and radio news departments on story about special security precautions. Schedule interviews with your spokesperson. Rehearse talking points and sound bites with spokesperson.
- On October 7 (one week before event), use your fact sheet to pitch TV and radio news departments on story about special security precautions. Schedule interviews with your spokesperson. Rehearse talking points and sound bites with spokesperson.
- By October 10 (four days before event), meet with event spokespersons to discuss on-site interview possibilities and rehearse potential questions and answers.

How Will You Bring This Together? Writing a Publicity Plan

171

> **Through the Ages Tactics** *continued*
>
> - Resend media alert October 11 (three days before event).
> - On October 13 (one day before event), call key media outlets to remind them of October 14 event. Resend media alerts if necessary. Assemble press kits to distribute to media at event.
> - On October 14 (morning of the event), call to confirm media attendance and provide name of on-site media coordinator. Arrive early with press kits to coordinate on-site interviews with President Bush before the dinner.

BUDGET FOR SUCCESS

Now that you know what you want to do, how does it fit with your organization's publicity budget? Do you have a realistic amount of money to spend? Can you get outside funding for your plan? Can you afford to hire an outside consultant for the work if you need to? What about volunteers? As noted in Chapter 1, the local chapter of the Public Relations Society of America (http://www.prsa.org) should be able to help you find a volunteer. Talk to a local college to find an intern who will work for just a few weeks if that's all you need for extra help. Networking can help you find public relations professionals who are willing to volunteer.

> ### Through the Ages Budget
>
> The publicity portion of the event promotion has no extra or unusual costs associated with it, but the event's marketing plan will have costs associated with invitation production and mailing.

PREPARE A TIMELINE

A timeline will help you manage the tasks and tactics included in your plan. If you want your op-ed to appear in a certain week to coincide with a local or national event, for example, then note both your start date and your targeted publication date on your timeline. If you plan to mail one press release a month, let your timeline reflect not only that schedule but when you need to start writing each release.

Use a format that works best for you. Some people like to use a month-by-month calendar; some like the historical timeline model; and others like to list the start date, the due date, the task, and the person responsible in a Word or Excel grid. Use whatever system will make certain that you execute the elements on time for maximum impact.

Through the Ages Timeline

April

Ongoing: Work as needed with speaker committee to make sure media interviews are included in speaker contract.

Ongoing: Work with event committee as needed for on-site media needs at dinner.

7: Write announcement news release, circulate for approval.

9-10: Update the media list.

14: Distribute announcement release. Get release approved for April 14 distribution.

22: Recruit publicity committee chair at board meeting.

May

Ongoing: Work with sponsorship committee to secure media sponsors representing print, radio, and television; negotiate in-kind trade—ads for sponsor identification.

22: Form publicity committee.

June

Date TBD: Provide information for ads by publication deadlines.

1: Begin recruiting TV personality as emcee.

1: Poll publicity committee on media connections.

2: Update media database with committee connections.

15: Have emcee on board.

Through the Ages Timeline *continued*

September

7: Write PSA scripts.

8: Update announcement release with new information and circulate for approval.

10: Begin contacting President Bush's representative to outline media relations plans.

14: Distribute PSA scripts to media.

14: Distribute second announcement release.

21: Pitch daily newspaper living section on article about elder abuse.

22: Start writing remaining press kit elements and circulate for approval.

28: Pitch daily newspaper local section on telephone interview with President Bush.

October

1: Finalize press kit.

6: Write and fax reminder media alert.

6: Write fact sheet listing special security precautions for the president's visit.

7: Pitch TV and radio on story about special security precautions, schedule interviews, and rehearse with spokesperson.

10: Meet with event spokespersons for update and rehearsal.

11: Resend media alert.

13: Remind media by phone.

13: Assemble press kits.

14: Call to confirm media attendance and provide name of on-site media coordinator.

14: Work with media on-site.

Use this worksheet to organize your thoughts.

Publicity Plan Worksheet

Situation/Overview

_____

_____

_____

_____

_____

Audiences

-
-
-

Goals

-
-
-

Strategy

_____

_____

_____

Tactics

-
-
-
-
-
-

Objectives

-
-
-
-
-
-

Budget
(Itemize estimated expenses; include staff time if appropriate.)

Timeline

Week/Month for Activity	Activity

KEEPING IT ALIVE

As you begin working with your plan, remember that it is fluid and flexible. You might find that one tactic is particularly effective at helping you reach your goals and decide to do more of that one. Be careful about abandoning one approach if it doesn't succeed right away, though. Publicity requires tenacity. Your news may not be used for many random reasons—there might have been too much competition for too little space that week, technology might have interfered with the delivery, or the media gatekeeper might have had a migraine when your information arrived. Much is beyond your control, which, again, differentiates "free" publicity from purchased advertising.

A lack of immediate success doesn't mean that you didn't have a good idea or that your execution was off. It just means that you need to keep trying. Veteran publicists say time after time that one secret to their success is persistence. They don't let defeat or an unpleasant experience deter them. They just keep putting it out there, knowing that if what they have is news, it will find a home and have an impact.

NEXT STEPS

Before moving on to learn more about hiring publicity consultants in the next chapter, take time to do the following:

- Write your publicity plan.
- Incorporate plan deadlines into your daily calendar system.
- Print the plan and keep it on your desk.

14

DO YOU NEED TO HIRE A PUBLICITY CONSULTANT?

You understand what publicity can accomplish for your organization and what it will take. You've got meaningful messages, and you know how to use the tools and tactics that will get these messages in front of your key audiences. But when it comes to publicity, the idea-generating process is often like going through the buffet line at a banquet—sometimes our eyes are bigger than our stomachs. It's time to ask yourself if you have the budget for your ideas as well as the staff to execute them. If you have the budget but not the staff, can you afford to hire an outside consultant? If you do, how do you select one? Here's how to figure out how to get the work done.

IN-HOUSE TALENT

Publicity requires certain skills, but not those of a nuclear physicist. If you have the luxury of assembling an in-house team, you want your organization's best writer, best salesperson, and most detail-oriented person. Your in-house writer need not be a novelist. If you have a small staff, you want the person who writes the best memos or always gets asked to write the annual report, even if it's not in their job description. Your salesperson might come from the development department. This individual should be comfortable picking up the phone and talking to a stranger about your organization. You will need this skill when pitching stories to the media. If you're planning a special event, recruit the staffer who is the most organized at meetings and who always manages to meet deadlines. This is somebody who knows how to make things happen.

The best full-time publicists have all of these skills. On the other hand, some are good at pitching but bad at writing. Others are great writers but can't keep track of project details or deadlines. What's *your* situation? If all of the work falls on your shoulders and you're a weak writer, take a class, workshop, or seminar that will help you improve your skills. You don't need to be a professional writer to handle publicity. You just need to write in a way that is clear and succinct and not overly promotional. If your best salesperson can't help out with the pitching, can this person teach you some of the tricks—how to overcome anxiety or reluctance or how to get to the point quickly? If you find it hard to stay on top of all of the details associated with event planning, investigate software that helps do that for you. Don't hesitate to use any kind of "crutch" to meet your objectives.

HIRING A CONSULTANT

If you don't have the internal resources to do the work or if the job is just too big for your staff, consider hiring an outside consultant. Look for an individual or an agency with public relations, not advertising, capability. Publicity and advertising, as explained in Chapter 1, are quite different and often require different skills, even though some people use the terms as if they're interchangeable.

Look into the possibility of an agency taking on your project on a pro bono basis. It's a reasonable option. Is there a service in your city that matches the communications needs of nonprofits with local professional communicators who donate their time? If not, network through local chapters of groups such as the Public Relations Society of America or the American Marketing Association to find out which agencies might take on pro bono projects to expand their portfolios.

If pro bono work isn't a good option, your first choice when paying for services is a public relations practitioner who is a sole proprietor or an agency that specializes in public relations assignments. That's where you'll find the most relevant experience. If your options are limited to agencies that do both advertising and public relations, look for those with staff dedicated to public relations activities—people who don't do any advertising work. People who are steeped in the advertising world often use too many superlatives. This, and a tendency to capitalize too many words, says to a reporter, "This isn't a news release, it's an advertisement." Reporters aren't interested in anything overly promotional.

Be wary of attempts from the advertising side to dominate the conversation, too. You're not coming to them for ads or a new Web site design. You want publicity. In addition, avoid talking to advertising agencies without publicity capabilities. You don't want to pay the staff to learn on the job—and regardless of what you might be told, there *is* a learning curve.

An experienced sole proprietor is often a good option if your assignment isn't too large or if the sole proprietor often contracts with freelancers for assistance on larger projects. "Solos" are often veterans who bring a great deal of experience to each project. Because their overhead is lower than that of a bigger firm, they often charge less for the same work while delivering a top-quality product. With a solo, you also know with whom you will be working—the owner, not a less experienced novice. These veteran publicists are often easy to work with, because their experience allows them to move forward independently once they're clear on what's expected. They don't require much guidance or hand-holding.

A small- to medium-sized firm can be a good choice, too, if it has the right talent and experience. These agencies have more depth, so you're not paying a senior level staffer a high rate to do clerical work. Most are adept at matching the task with the talent—and billing you accordingly.

WHERE TO FIND A CONSULTANT

Look for a communications consultant for your project the way you might search for an accountant or a lawyer—ask around. Talk to your board members for recommendations. Ask colleagues at other companies and nonprofit organizations whom they've worked with,

remembering to ask them whether they were satisfied with the results.
Talk to local reporters about whom they would recommend, because
the people who receive news releases, e-mails, and telephone pitches
are in an excellent position to tell you who does the best job. They can
also tell you who does the worst job—so don't forget to ask them about
that, too.

The local chapter of the Public Relations Society of America is another excellent resource. The president, always a local practitioner,
should be able to give you contact information for a few members who
can handle your assignment. Go to http://www.prsa.org/Chapters/vie-
wall/index.cfm to find your local chapter. The phone book will help you
uncover local consultants or firms, and Internet searches will help you
learn more from their Web sites. While Web sites won't provide you with
input or endorsements from people you know, they should be able to
help you learn more about the clients and projects of various agencies.
The design of a firm's Web site provides valuable insight into how well
the agency communicates, too. Is the type too tiny to read? Is the site
heavy on graphics and light on text? Is it easy to find out how to contact
them? If you find yourself frustrated as you try to get information on a
firm's Web site—which is not unusual with advertising agency sites—then

that agency probably isn't your best choice. You want a firm that excels at communicating with words, not pictures.

PICK UP THE PHONE

After you've done this small amount of legwork to identify a few solo practitioners or agencies (five to seven is a good start) that come highly recommended, call them. If your referral sources have given you the name of an individual, start there. If not, ask for the president. Briefly explain your situation and the services you're looking for, then ask if the agency does that kind of work well. Some will be honest and say they don't. Use that opportunity to ask who does, getting a contact name and phone number if possible. Others will say they are a good fit for you—and they are—while still others will tell you they excel at what you need even if they don't. Your evaluation process will help you zero in on the firm that has the most relevant experience and can get the results you're looking for.

Send each firm on your final list a briefing letter that describes your organization and its work and provides more detail about your project. In addition to the project description, offer information on the audiences you're trying to reach, your publicity goals, and your budget range. In return, ask them to respond with their own letter that presents the agency's overall background, its experience with communications situations similar to yours, a short overview of work it has done for other nonprofit organizations, a description of its staff, and its fee structure. Request background materials that help demonstrate capabilities.

You might find resistance to this, with agencies responding that the information is on their Web site or that they'll send a brochure instead. That's not enough. You need a response letter because it's the only way you'll be able to compare agencies fairly. Not all firms put the same information on their Web sites or in their promotional materials, and most don't state their fee structure in any of those materials. In addition, clicking through Web sites or hunting for specific information in a brochure requires a fair amount of effort on your part. Put the onus on them to convince you they have the ability to do your work. Those who are unwilling to spend the small amount of time to send you a capabilities letter are probably not seriously interested in working with you.

Review all the responses for any immediate conclusions—is the firm too small or too large? Does it lack publicity experience all together? Does it lack experience with nonprofit organizations? Is it sloppy, uninformative, or disorganized? Use the Public Relations Agency Evaluation Grid (a worksheet that can be photocopied is included in the Appendix) to record your impressions for each agency in as many grid categories as you can. Which ones score low enough to be eliminated? Use the grids first to identify which firms don't have the right qualifications, then to help you decide which you'd like to meet personally.

Public Relations Agency Evaluation Grid

Agency: _____

Quality or characteristic	How important is this quality to your company or the project, on a scale of 1 to 5? (1 is the lowest, 5 is the highest)	How do you rank the agency for this quality on a scale of 1 to 5? (1 is the lowest, 5 is the highest)
Agency size		
Overall publicity and public relations capability		
Media relations experience		
Writing skills		
In-person communication skills		
Knowledge of your field		
Experience working with nonprofit organizations		
Whether the agency was referred to you by more than one source		
Your impression of its ability to meet deadlines		
Creativity		
Chemistry with your group		
Reputation		
TOTAL OF ALL ROWS		

MEET IN PERSON

Schedule in-person meetings with the firms you'd like to get to know, and call or write to those with whom you won't be meeting to let them know that, while you appreciated learning more about them, you're pursuing opportunities elsewhere. When scheduling the meetings, tell each agency what you're expecting: a capabilities presentation that tells you theirs is the best firm for the job and an opportunity for you to meet in person the people with whom you would be working. The latter point is almost as important as the first. You want to make sure not only that you're comfortable working with the person you'll be dealing with the most, but that you have the sense the person has the ability and experience to do the job. This is so important, in fact, that if you are unable for whatever reason to meet the person who will be doing your work, you will want to make your contract contingent upon a successful meeting between you and that person. You need to be certain you like, trust, and respect the person you'll be working with on a daily basis.

As for capabilities, specify that you want the presentation to demonstrate that they've had success with this type of assignment before. You aren't looking for a general capabilities presentation. You want the remarks to address experiences specific to your assignment. Let the agency know that your meeting can't exceed 90 minutes, including discussion and questions and answers.

Allow 90 minutes for each agency, but schedule the meetings back-to-back in two-hour blocks. That gives you enough time to move the representative out the door before the competition arrives for the next appointment, while also giving you a little time to catch your breath between sessions.

The goal of each meeting—besides showing you if the representative can follow instructions—is to help you decide which agency would do a good job for you. Look for chemistry—do you like the people you're meeting? Review samples of their work. Is it high quality? Are they offering proof that they can do what you're asking? Or do you get the sense that they are all hype and no substance? Be careful about being misled by razzle-dazzle presentations that are impressive but don't say much. Look closely at that sole proprietor whose dog-and-pony show can't compare to that of a larger agency but who is highly recommended and has done similar work to what you need. What did you think of the questions that person asked of you? Did it show they had absorbed what you provided in your briefing letter or that they did additional research to get a little smarter? Or did you get the impression that you weren't "heard?"

After each meeting, complete the remainder of each agency's evaluation grid. Tally the points and see if there's a clear winner. If not—if they all seem quite comparable—put your bet on the firm that has the best publicity track record. If that firm has been doing publicity well for some time, it's likely they won't disappoint you. But before calling the "winner" with the good news, check references. Ask clients or former clients what they liked best about the firm, what they liked least, and if they would hire them again. Ask what the agency does best and where it needs improvement. Factor this information into your decision-making process, using the feedback, your grid, and your gut to help you select the right choice for your project.

Notify all agencies of your decision. Then schedule a meeting with the agency you're hiring. Review your publicity plan with them and get their reaction. Do they agree that your plan will take you where you want to go? Would they make changes? Don't let them take you off course without a convincing argument, but do give them a chance to shape the plan into something they feel comfortable executing.

Create a document that outlines what the consultant will be doing and what it will cost. If fees don't match your budget, ask what can be done with the budget you have. Note, however, that you provided a budget range in you briefing letter, so a final execution that deviates significantly from that could be a red flag, leading you to reconsider working with that firm.

Once you've agreed on the assignment and fee, request a detailed letter of agreement that outlines what each organization is responsible for providing or creating, the time frame of the assignment, what the work will cost, payment terms, and cancellation terms.

HOW ARE AGENCIES PAID?

While advertising agencies make their money by collecting a percentage of ad spending or marking up printing or other expenses, public relations agencies charge an hourly rate for their time. Project fees are based on the hourly rates of the people working on the project multiplied by the project's estimated hours. Rates vary widely, depending on the market and the experience of the people at the firm. While rates can range anywhere from $50 to $500 per hour, a realistic range is more like $75 to $250. Firms charge separately for expenses. Some mark them up, while others don't. Make sure expenses are included in the budget you agreed on, not added after the fact.

There are a number of fee arrangements; your agency will tell you how they usually handle this. Some bill hours as the work is done through a monthly invoice. Many clients like this approach, because they are only paying for the work actually done that month. If you use this method, make sure there is a ceiling on the number of hours the agency is allowed to bill on the project and that they notify you when they approach that ceiling. You don't want any surprises. In addition, you want assurances from the agency that, even if they underestimated how many hours the assignment would take, they will still complete the job without penalizing you for their mistake.

Others estimate the amount of time a project will take and charge a flat fee, regardless of the number of hours actually spent when the project is done. In these situations, they often ask for one-third of the fee to start the work, one-third midway through, and one-third upon completion. This works best with short-term projects, lasting three months or less. Still others divide the fee among the number of months required for the project, call it a retainer, and bill the same amount at the beginning or end of each month. Retainers work better for some than for others. Some clients are uncomfortable paying the same fee for a slow month as they do for a busy month, even though the work all averages out in the end. Others like that they know how much they'll be paying each month.

In recent years, the number of "pay for placement" agencies has increased. These firms charge a flat fee for media placements based on the type of media outlet and the market size. This is an appropriate option only for media relations campaigns. On the one hand, if the firm doesn't have any success, you're charged only the "set-up" fee. On the other hand, if the agency does a bang-up job, you could be paying more for the results than if you used a publicist who only charges by the hour. Approach this nontraditional billing concept with caution.

Select the approach that works best for both your organization and the agency so that you feel you're paying fairly and they feel they're compensated in a timely enough manner.

All of this should be included in your letter of agreement. Make certain, too, that the agreement stipulates that the agency does not charge you beyond the estimate, unless the nature of the assignment changes and you approve the increased budget in writing. Too many clients are surprised by invoices that exceed the agreed-upon estimate; too many agencies don't understand the problems caused by invoice surprises. These relationships aren't unlike marriages, where arguments over money top the list of marital issues. Just as in marriage, keeping the lines of communication open helps make any financial issues more manageable.

MANAGING EXPECTATIONS

Once the honeymoon is over, what can you realistically expect from your agency? Don't expect miracles—not that you would have hired a firm that promised them. You also wouldn't have hired a firm that guaranteed their results, because as you've learned from this book, with publicity there are *no* guarantees. What you can expect is an agency that leads the process with wisdom and experience. You should expect advice and reasonable results that are documented in a way that allows you to showcase them internally. You can expect to work with bright, creative people who realize that their job is to make you look good. If they make you look *bad*, you've got a problem.

From an administrative perspective, your agency should be at least a step ahead of you, reminding you what information is needed or what document is due back from the approval process, not the other way around. You should expect to work with people who know when to ask questions—who know what they don't know. You should expect that the material that comes to you for approval is as flawless as they can make it. Yes, you'll find an occasional typo or misspelling, but not more than 1 or 2 in a 500-word news release. Have a conversation about quality control if mistakes become a pattern. You can also expect that, when representing you with any of your stakeholders, your agency behaves in an appropriately professional manner.

Your agency team has expectations, too. It expects you to provide the information, intelligence, and support it needs to do the job as expected. Agencies are often disappointed when they start a new relationship with great enthusiasm, only to discover that the client isn't accessible enough, ignores deadlines, or doesn't facilitate necessary introductions in-house. Be sensitive to the fact that the busiest among us can sometimes become roadblocks to progress because we can't find our way through the pile of materials on our desks. Publicity is a very time-sensitive business, requiring careful attention to deadlines and, sometimes, an immediate turnaround. The only way to facilitate a fast turnaround is to make it a priority. Talking to your agency at the start of your relationship about what you will need from each other on a daily or weekly basis will help you identify and avoid potential problems.

NEXT STEPS

Before moving on to the next chapter, which explains how to evaluate your publicity success, take time to do the following:

- Decide if you need to hire an outside consultant.
- If you do, begin networking as soon as possible to discover who's good at publicity and who isn't.
- Talk to those you're considering, send them a briefing letter, and request a capabilities letter in return.
- Schedule in-person meetings with those firms whose capabilities fit your needs.
- Select an agency for the right reasons—their experience is relevant, their work is good, you feel you can work with the staff, and they're affordable.
- Avoid surprises by putting everything in writing—who will do what and when, what it will cost, and when they will be paid.

15

HOW WILL YOU EVALUATE YOUR SUCCESS?

It's hard to measure the impact of publicity, yet it needs to be done. Tracking and studying the results of your publicity efforts allows you to identify patterns and learn from your experiences. It helps you make decisions for future campaigns. And it helps you make sure the time and energy that go into your publicity programs take you where you want to go. The problem, though, is that change caused by free media exposure is often hard to separate from change or action caused by advertising, direct mail, and other marketing efforts. Advertising and direct mail offer tangible ways to track impact—coupons are a good example—so it's easier to link behavior to promotional triggers.

What makes it even harder to determine publicity's role in a program's success is the fact that so many people don't understand the difference between publicity and advertising. Ask a caller how they heard about your organization, and they might say, "I saw your ad in the newspaper." When you're not buying any advertising, that response is confusing. What they meant, though, was that they saw an *article* about your organization in the newspaper. This kind of confusion means that, even if you ask people to indicate how they heard about something, you won't know if what inspired them really was your publicity, your advertising, or your Web site for that matter. It's all interchangeable in the minds of people who don't work with these words and tools every day.

Still, there are ways to determine if your publicity is helping you move forward. You can also do some things to make sure your publicity success is seen and appreciated by internal audiences, too.

TRACKING SYSTEMS

You can't evaluate your success without first setting up a system that tracks your activities and monitors the outcome. The system you use depends on the nature of your program, but what you gain from your system should always be the same. You want to be able to tell at a glance where you're having the most and least success. If your program is complex, incorporating a range of tactics supporting various initiatives, consider setting up your tracking system by tactic: pitching story ideas, sending op-eds to the press, and so on. This system will let you see first how each tactic fared so you can compare one tactic to another and see if one was more successful. If your organization has never done publicity before and you're starting out slowly with news releases or tip sheets, your system will be simpler but just as meaningful.

For many, an Excel spreadsheet or a Word table or grid works well. Perhaps you have contact management software that generates the summary reports you need. Let the approach in Table 15.1 give you ideas about what format would work best for your work style, tools, and publicity plans. What does Table 15.1 tell you about the outcome of one tactic? First, it was very successful, as you see by the number of placements and potential reach. Second, it reveals that the television news departments are competitive. One station didn't want the story when it learned that another station had picked it up, while a third agreed to do a related segment but not the same piece as the first station. It also tells you that the weekly newspaper is more likely than the daily to use the entire tip sheet.

What can you learn from this? Perhaps that you want to make sure the weekly newspaper is always on your media distribution list; that you need to pitch ideas to the TV news dpartments one at a time, moving on to the second with the idea only after the first has rejected it; and that your daily newspaper definitely considers this type of information

TABLE 15.1 *Publicity Tracking Chart*

Tactic	Date	Media Outlet	Circulation/ Reach	Next Steps	Result	Result Date
Tip sheet: Five ways to sing like an opera diva	Jan. 15	*Daily Gazette*	170,000	Called for singer's head shot	Column note with singer's head shot	Jan. 20
		Weekly Journal	22,000		Ran full tip sheet	Jan. 23
		Channel 3	250,000	Schedule singer for in-studio demonstration for morning news	Singer taught morning news host how to do it	Jan. 20
		Channel 5			Not interested because Ch. 3 picked it up first	
		Channel 7	175,000	Schedule interview with artistic director to talk about this year's season	Interview ran on noon news program	Jan. 21
Tactic summary		**4 placements**	**Potential reach: 617,000**			

newsworthy. It's easy to see the value of logging and tracking your activities when you put it into a system that shows what happened.

The importance of tracking also highlights why you need to stay on top of who's using what. It's not as easy as it looks—if you've given them good materials to work from, they might not call you for an interview, more information, photos, or anything else. They'll use what you sent without telling you and move on to the next item. This is more likely to be true with the print outlets than broadcast, though, because broadcast often relies on interviews or other video footage. The point is, you need to either scan your media outlets continually while in publicity mode or pay a media monitoring service to do so. If you're only seeking local publicity, it's best to do the monitoring yourself. It's less expensive than hiring a service, and you want to monitor the press regularly anyway as you learn more about what types of news and information they use. In addition, don't you want to be the first to announce that the organization is in the newspaper that morning?

Another alternative for regional or national publicity programs is to search for clips on a site like NewsLibrary (http://www.newslibrary.com), which scans hundreds of daily newspapers, then charges a small fee to deliver the entire item. (This service is useful when you're researching a topic or issue, too.) In some cases, you can use what you've learned on that site to go directly to the newspaper's site to see if the article is available for free. But because some newspapers are selective about what content they put online and others archive content quickly and charge a fee for archive access, you have to act quickly to save money by securing clips yourself.

Several media monitoring or clipping services will provide this service, charging both a monthly scanning and per clipping fee. These services are particularly useful for national or regional campaigns, when you need to monitor results but can't do it all yourself, or with satellite offices or chapters. They are also useful when you need to get a videotape of an interview rather than a transcript. Some of the better known services include Bacon's Information (http://www.bacons.com); Burrelles Luce (http://www.burrellesluce.com); CyberAlert (http://www.cyberalert.com); eWatch from PRNewswire (http://ewatch.prnewswire.com); Video Monitoring Services of America (http://www.vidmon.com); multivision (http://www.multivisioninc.com); and Metro Monitor (http://www.metromonitor.com). Many of the services are highly sophisticated, delivering clips electronically and providing tools that let you evaluate the exposure and prepare reports.

Prices range from $195 per month for Web and broadcast monitoring to around $150 per month to monitor all media outlets in one state and more than $300 per month for national coverage. Clippings, videotapes, and DVDs are usually extra. They are valuable resources for large organizations with nationwide programs, issues, and activities to monitor.

WHAT'S THE VALUE?

There are many ways to determine the value of your campaign, but the method you choose should help you determine if you reached your goals and objectives. If your goal was to change attitudes or raise awareness, the only way you would know if you "moved the needle" would be to conduct pre-campaign research to define awareness, attitudes, or opinions about your organization or issue. When your publicity program ends, you would conduct post-campaign research to determine whether the program had an impact on awareness or attitudes.

But so many other possible goals require different evaluation methods that might or might not allow you to draw conclusions. If your goal was to increase ticket sales to an annual fundraising dinner by 20 percent, you'll know the night of the event if you did indeed sell as many tickets as you hoped. But how much of that was due to your publicity versus event advertising, direct mail, and word of mouth? It is impossible to tell. On the other hand, it's logical to assume that if you met the targets outlined in your publicity objectives, your work contributed to the event's success.

One evaluation approach to use if your goal is to influence or sway opinions involves analyzing the quality of the content of your media exposure. Look through your clippings, videotapes, and audiotapes for your communications messages. Were they used? Did the clips communicate what you wanted them to? Did they get your point across? Was the media coverage positive or negative, flattering or unflattering? If the topic was controversial, did your viewpoint come through? If it centered around an issue that people were for or against, did the tone of the coverage seem to support your view or the other side's?

Use content analysis to help determine if you need to make adjustments in how you communicate through the media, too. Did you get publicity but your messages were missing? Maybe you need to rewrite them to communicate more clearly or make them more quotable or usable. Did you get your topic covered, but the coverage was almost universally inaccurate? Figure out how to improve the information you're sharing so it's not misunderstood or misinterpreted. Did you schedule many interviews with your spokesperson, but the person was never quoted? Maybe you need to do some media training or use a different individual for media interviews.

If your goals and objectives were built around the timing or quantity of the desired publicity, look to see if you met those goals. Did you get the publicity when you wanted it? Did you get as much as you needed?

Some people evaluate the success of their program on what it would have cost to purchase that media space or time if it had been considered

---

Turnkey **P**rogram **Y**ields **R**esults

To attract middle school teachers to Yellowstone National Park's electronic field trip Web site (*http://www.windowsintowonderland.org*), Smith and Dress, Ltd. created a turnkey program that would allow one middle school in each targeted market to serve as an education partner for the district, communicate the model internally to science teachers, and coordinate local media for a demonstration. The firm worked closely with district public relations officers to coordinate publicity, providing them with a news release, photos from the Web site, a video news release and B-roll video footage of Yellowstone National Park. By using the firm-supplied materials, schools got "good news" publicity when local newspapers sent reporters and photographers to cover the individual class e-trips. The success of the program in the initial ten districts has allowed it to expand to other U.S. cities, bringing media attention to the schools, to the park, and to its corporate sponsor, Canon.

---

advertising. This is most relevant if this is how you established your goals—"To generate the equivalent of $125,000 worth of advertising." On the other hand, when a campaign secures a lot of publicity, the advertising value can be impressive. If using this somewhat tedious, time-consuming approach, work with sales representatives of the various media outlets to determine the costs of paid media exposure.

With annual events, make comparisons with those of previous years. Now that you're making a concerted effort to generate publicity, is attendance up? Did you raise more money? Did contributions increase for a period after the event?

MAKE SURE IT GETS NOTICED

When evaluating the impact of your publicity efforts, don't forget to take into account its impact on internal audiences too—your leadership, colleagues, volunteers, board of directors, constituents, and others you work with. The best way to make sure it has made an impact, of course, is to share your success as quickly as possible. Circulate clippings internally as soon as you get them—make sure the article from this morning's newspaper is on the boss's desk as soon as she gets to her office. If somebody from your organization will be interviewed on that evening's newscast, send an e-mail to staff and others so they know to watch, too.

Get permission to reprint especially good articles or organization profiles on your Web site. Include information about your media relations success in your marketing and volunteer newsletters. Work closely with the development staff to get them clippings in a format that's useful for their purposes, too.

Prepare a summary report on each program's publicity support and circulate it with staff and at the board of directors meeting. While your ultimate goal is to raise the visibility of your organization or cause, you also want to make sure that the decision makers in your organization understand the impact of your publicity efforts. The more they see publicity's impact, the more valuable they'll feel it is—and the more resources you'll have to develop and nurture those important media relationships that will help your organization, grow, thrive, and succeed.

NEXT STEPS

Before moving on to the next chapter to learn about additional marketing options, take time to do the following:

- Set up a tracking system.
- Determine which evaluation method will allow you to match your results with your goals and objectives.
- Decide how to leverage your publicity successes within your organization and among key audiences.

16

WHAT OTHER PROMOTIONAL TACTICS WILL YOU USE?

Marketing is promoting what you provide to your constituents. Publicity can help you promote your products or services, but in many cases, especially in fundraising situations, it can't do it alone. Other promotional methods you'll rely on include direct mail, advertising, public speaking, a Web site, an electronic newsletter, and viral marketing, among others.

How do they differ from each other and what can you accomplish with each? All give you more control than publicity—but they also cost more. Advertising lets you control the message sent to the same audience you might reach through publicity. Direct mail and an electronic newsletter are more targeted, allowing you to reach a very specific audience when you need to, saying exactly what you want to say. A Web site makes your information available to anybody, anytime. Public speaking lets you reach out in a personal way to smaller audiences. Viral marketing is unpredictable and depends on the kindness of strangers—but when it happens, it's great. Here's what you need to know about each to help you decide which mix is best for your organization's needs.

DIRECT MAIL IS MORE TARGETED

Direct mail is printed material sent directly through the mail to prospective customers or contributors. It's a valuable technique used by nonprofit organizations to solicit donations, recruit volunteers, inform a target audience about products or services, invite people to special events, and so on. Direct mail begins with understanding who you want to reach, what you want to say to them, and how to say it effectively. It involves a good mailing list and a written communications piece that is suitable for the purpose and the audience.

Nonprofit organizations using direct mail to entice shoppers to a retail component, such as a thrift shop, will get their greatest success with a special offer, such as a discount with purchase. In general, however, much of the success of direct mail hinges on the mailing list. All nonprofit organizations should maintain an internal database of donors and prospects. This shouldn't limit them to communicating only with the people on that list when using direct mail, though. When reaching out to a new audience, rent a list from a list broker or partner with a business that is already mailing to your target audience. It's not unusual, for example, for the local power company to include a flyer from a nonprofit organization with its residential bills.

That in-house list is still very important, though. Make maintaining, updating, and expanding your in-house database a priority. Use first class for bulk mailings periodically, so the envelopes with bad addresses get returned and you can purge the names from your system. Always look for opportunities to expand your list, not only by adding new donors and volunteers but by soliciting addresses when hosting a booth at a health fair or similar event or getting signatures on a petition; by adding event registrants (such as participants in a charity race, for example); and by capturing contact information from people who call to inquire about your services. At the same time, make sure you have a procedure in place for removing people from the list when they request that you do so.

Direct mail programs can be very simple or very complicated, depending on what you're trying to achieve, whom you're trying to reach, the size of your budget, and so on. Sophisticated direct marketers test, test, and then retest their various direct mail components: the text of the letter, special offer, list, teaser copy on the mailing envelope, what the address on the envelope looks like . . . the list goes on and on. While it is difficult for a small, local nonprofit organization to apply a high level of sophistication to its direct mail campaigns, testing as much as possible to maximize your impact is still wise. Several books on direct mail for nonprofits tell you how.

ADVERTISING OFFERS MORE CONTROL THAN PUBLICITY DOES

Advertising might be the promotional technique nonprofit organizations are most familiar with. It is less targeted than direct mail, resulting in more waste, yet it can reach interested people who for one reason or another will never be on your mailing list. Use advertising wisely and cautiously and only after first exhausting nonpaid options, such as publicity. Public service announcements—PSAs—are essentially advertisements you haven't paid for, so work to secure image, issue, or event exposure through PSAs before buying an ad. But since you can't be guaranteed the exposure you need through a PSA because you don't control if or when it is used, you'll want to use advertising to support events requiring ticket purchases.

One of the advantages of advertising is that, once you know who you want to reach and what you want to say, you can get all the information you need to make a decision about where to advertise from the media outlets themselves. Advertising sales representatives are well armed with information about reach and costs. Use their information about circulation, audience, and costs to make an informed decision about which outlet does the best job of reaching your target audience (and use this information for publicity purposes, too). While they will advise you on how many times you need to run your ad—frequency—your budget will decide how often you can afford to advertise.

The media outlets—even small weekly newspapers—have the talent in-house to create your advertisements. There will be production charges in some situations, but for the most part, you will get a cost-effective, well-executed advertisement from your media partner. An alternative is to align with an advertising agency that donates its services pro bono in exchange for the opportunity to develop its portfolio or give its employees more meaningful work. While this collaboration might be an excellent opportunity, be alert to two potential pitfalls. First, some advertising agencies seek pro bono work as an opportunity to develop the kind of "award-winning" material that clients often won't allow. That's because the creative work that wins advertising awards is often evaluated on its visual appeal, not its success at communicating effectively. Second, a nonprofit organization that is soliciting contributions needs to be careful that its materials don't look so slick that they suggest the organization doesn't really need the money it's requesting.

PUBLIC SPEAKING GETS PERSONAL

Speaking to a group about your cause or issue is an excellent, cost-effective way to reach a targeted audience with your messages. Begin by looking for groups that represent your stakeholders. If you're seeking upscale women, you might find an audience among the women's groups formed at country clubs or at Junior League meetings. If you're targeting business owners, look for local entrepreneurial groups such as a National Association of Women Business Owners chapter or the Young Presidents' Organization. It takes a little effort to identify who plans the monthly meetings and selects the speakers for these groups, but a few phone calls and e-mails usually pay off.

When you have a target list of groups and contacts, decide on a presentation title for each, because what is appropriate for one might not work for another. If you're comfortable making a telephone pitch, call the group's meeting planner to pitch your presentation idea. That person can decide if it will work as is or will need some tweaking and will suggest subsequent steps. You can accomplish the same goal with a short e-mail. If you choose to send a letter by mail, go into more detail about the presentation than you would in a telephone or e-mail pitch.

After your concept has been accepted, your presentation is scheduled, and you know how long you'll be speaking, send the meeting planner a program description for the meeting notice or the group's newsletter, your speaker introduction, and your audiovisual needs. A few days before the meeting date, call the planner to learn how many people are attending so you bring enough handouts. And you *do* want to use handouts. These leave-behinds provide an opportunity for you to extend the reach of your message while providing attendees with contact information they can use to schedule you as a speaker at another group's meeting.

When preparing your remarks, avoid the tendency to share everything you believe the audience needs to know about your cause. What's your most important point? Build your presentation around that one point by telling stories that illustrate your message. Stories help people remember your messages. Begin by telling them what you're going to tell them, tell them, and end by telling them what you told them. Providing focus and this type of structure will make it easier for your audience to absorb and remember what's most important.

Finally, take the time to practice, practice, practice until you are comfortable with your material. Practice and rehearse until you are familiar enough with your presentation to speak from an outline rather than a script. You will make more of an impact—and make a stronger connection with the audience—if you aren't reading prepared remarks.

ELECTRONIC NEWSLETTERS ARE QUICK AND EASY

If you haven't launched an electronic newsletter yet, now's the time to do so, *if* the people with whom you want to communicate use e-mail regularly. E-newsletters are less expensive, more timely, and easier to create than their print counterparts.

While you probably receive many nicely designed e-newsletters, it's wise to use the simplest format possible—text only—to make sure that all recipients can view and read it properly. Publish quarterly, at a minimum, to make it worth your while. Many groups find that monthly is a workable frequency. Avoid filling each issue with promotional messages. Instead, focus on information readers can use or learn from so that they see your organization as a trusted expert on your issue. An organization that works to keep taxes from going up might want to solicit donations in its newsletter, for example, but it shouldn't make donations the focus. Instead, it can offer a short but thoughtful article about one way to reduce taxes before inserting that request for contributions. If you sometimes have difficulty generating content ideas, solicit informative articles from outside contributors.

Make sure you have the permission of recipients to add them to your distribution list. Do this either by making it clear when you gather e-mail addresses that you will be using them for a newsletter, or, if you have an e-mail list already, by sending the first issue with a highlighted message explaining how they can get themselves removed from the distribution list.

While e-newsletters are easy to distribute—you can send your publication to a distribution list of hundreds or thousands simultaneously with just a few mouse clicks—that same feature presents problems. Some Internet service providers block messages that are mass-mailed. To prevent this, you can self-distribute in small batches or use one of the many free newsletter distribution services that have this all figured out. These include NotifyList.com (http://www.notifylist.com); Yahoo (http://groups.yahoo.com); and EzineDirector (http://www.ezinedirector.com). Also, check with your Internet service provider to see if it offers this service. It might already be included in your monthly fee.

VIRAL MARKETING CAN BE CONTAGIOUS

Viral marketing is any marketing technique that encourages an individual to spread your message to friends, colleagues, family, and others. The term is misleading because it reminds us of those Internet viruses we're so afraid of. The idea behind viral marketing, though, is to create a campaign that becomes as "contagious" as a virus.

You can create a viral campaign that spreads the word about your organization in several ways. The first is to include a message in your e-newsletter that says, "Please feel free to forward this newsletter to others who might find it interesting." If you have 500 people on your distribution list and they each send it to 3 people, you've just reached an additional 1,500 people. This gives your newsletter a third-party endorsement from a friend that makes it more likely to be read by the recipient, who might not read unsolicited mail coming directly from you. People won't forward information that isn't interesting or useful, though, so make sure that e-newsletter is informational, not sales-oriented or promotional.

Make certain that your informational e-mail messages—particularly your e-newsletters—focus on content that is interesting and useful. Include material that readers will want to share with others. Let it showcase what you do best in a way that helps or informs others. Recipients can't help but want to share your messages when they contain information others will want to know.

Get your Web site working for you, too. Ask your Web designer to include a button on your Web site that says, "Send this page to a friend." Again, the message is sent by a friend rather than by your organization, giving the message more credibility. Make certain you have an opt-in mechanism on your Web site for that new viewer to enter an e-mail address to receive your e-newsletter, too. That also gives you a new contact for your potential donor database.

NEXT STEPS

Before reviewing the Appendix materials, take time to do the following:

- Decide which of these additional promotional techniques meet your needs.
- Research them in greater depth through Internet topic searches or by reading any of the many books on each technique.
- Incorporate those with the greatest potential into your promotion plan.

SAMPLE TOOLS

(Sample news release)

CONTACT: Jan Beckwith
(phone number)
(e-mail address)

SPAY/NEUTER GROUP RETURNS
AFFORDABLE VETERINARY CARE TO FITCHBURG

FITCHBURG, MA—August 22, 2005—Second Chance Fund for Animal Welfare, Inc. has announced plans to open a veterinary clinic in Fitchburg, potentially closing the gap created when the Fitchburg Animal Clinic went out of business in February. The new clinic, Second Chance Veterinary Clinic, will be only the third nonprofit veterinary clinic in the state.

Second Chance Fund, a 501(c)3 nonprofit that services Worcester County homeless cats and pet dogs and cats suffering from abuse, abandonment, disease, and lack of care, intends to open the clinic at 339 Broad Street, behind Crocker Field. The building would also be the group's headquarters.

Jan Beckwith, president and founder of Second Chance Fund, said she was already looking for a headquarters building when the Fitchburg clinic closed. That gap in care for more than 5,000 pet owners in the area spurred her to look in Fitchburg for space that would house both a clinic and her growing organization. "We are thrilled at the opportunity this presents for us to expand our reach to more animals in need while resurrecting affordable veterinary care in Fitchburg," she said.

Before Second Chance Fund can move into its new space, however, such use of the property needs the city's approval. "The first thing we will do is request a permit modification from the city's Planning Board," she said. The group must also raise $100,000 to convert the existing manufacturing facility into a clinic. Funding is expected to come from private donors, foundations, fraternal organizations, and bank loans. Beckwith asks that interested donors visit www.secondchancefund.org for more information, or send contributions to SCFAW, PO Box 118, Bolton, MA 01740.

Second Chance Fund for Animal Welfare, Inc. works to decrease the suffering of homeless cats and pet dogs and cats in Worcester County. In the past four years, the organization has spayed or neutered more than 4,000 feral, stray, and domestic cats and dogs through its trap-neuter-release and Quick Fix Clinics and found homes for almost 1,000 cats and kittens.

Reprinted with permission of Second Chance Fund for Animal Welfare, Inc.

(Sample news release)

NASHER SCULPTURE CENTER TO OPEN IN DALLAS, TEXAS, OCTOBER 2003

New Public Sculpture Center and Garden to Feature One of the Foremost Collections of Modern Sculpture

Innovative Indoor-Outdoor Gallery and Garden Facility Designed by Renzo Piano

Dallas, TX—The Nasher Sculpture Center, opening on October 20, 2003, will be the first institution in the world dedicated exclusively to the exhibition of modern and contemporary sculpture with a collection of global significance as its foundation. The Nasher Sculpture Center is further distinguished by a groundbreaking facility and landscaped garden specifically designed for the indoor and outdoor display of sculpture. Conceived by collector and philanthropist Raymond D. Nasher in consultation with museum professionals and scholars, the $70 million Center will occupy a full city block in downtown Dallas, in the heart of the city's growing Arts District.

The Nasher Sculpture Center will feature a new 54,000-square-foot-building and one and a half-acre sculpture garden designed by architect Renzo Piano in collaboration with landscape architect Peter Walker. The Center will provide a public home for the presentation of the Raymond and Patsy Nasher Collection, one of the foremost collections of modern sculpture in public or private hands and comprised of more than 300 sculptures dating from the late 19th century to the present.

"The Nasher Sculpture Center is the first institution to place modern and contemporary sculpture at the center of attention, with the collection, resources, and facilities to support such a focus," says Mr. Nasher. "Our goal in creating this institution is to concurrently foster the public enjoyment of sculpture and advance study in the field, two things very important to me and my late wife Patsy."

Distinguished by its remarkable range and depth, the Nasher Collection features work by 19th-century masters such as Auguste Rodin, Edgar Degas, and Paul Gauguin, to that of contemporary artists including Richard Serra and Mark di Suvero. Particularly notable are the comprehensive representations of seminal works by Pablo Picasso (seven sculptures),

Henri Matisse (11), Alberto Giacometti (13), Henry Moore (eight), Joan Miró (four), and David Smith (eight), as well as less renowned, yet highly inventive sculptors, such as Medardo Rosso, Raymond Duchamp-Villon, and Willem de Kooning.

Drawing on the breadth and continued growth of the Nasher Collection, installations in the Nasher Sculpture Center's galleries and gardens will be rotated periodically. The Center will also present a broad scope of public programming, including exhibitions organized by the institution and major touring exhibitions, as well as educational outreach programs and performing arts presentations.

"As the first institution of its kind, we are carefully developing a program that will build upon and complement existing research activities," remarks Dr. Steven Nash, Director of the Nasher Sculpture Center. "Collaborating with arts institutions and universities in the U.S. and worldwide, our goal is to create a dynamic environment that serves all audiences."

Located in the heart of the downtown Arts District, the Nasher Sculpture Center will occupy a 2.4-acre site adjacent to the Dallas Museum of Art and the Morton H. Meyerson Symphony Center. The collaborative relationship between the Center and neighboring institutions will be a model for collection-sharing and programmatic partnerships between arts organizations. The Dallas Museum of Art's outstanding holdings of modern and contemporary art, and encyclopedic permanent collection, will complement and provide context for the Nasher Collection. The Center has already collaborated with the Dallas Symphony Orchestra on the three-year loan of *Proverb*, by Mark di Suvero. The 60-foot-high red steel sculpture, installed next to the Morton H. Meyerson Symphony Center, creates a prominent gateway to the Dallas Arts District.

The Building and Garden

The main floor of the 54,000-square-foot building is divided into five equal-sized, parallel pavilions. The side walls are clad in two-inch wide slabs of Italian travertine, entirely concealing the facility's environmental and security systems and providing a quiet setting for the presentation of sculpture. The facades at each end are fabricated from clear glass, allowing the pavilions to visually extend into the garden and creating a seamless continuity between the Center's indoor and outdoor spaces. A unique barrel-vaulted glass ceiling is suspended above the galleries, atop narrow steel ribs and supported by thin, stainless steel rods. An innovative cast aluminum sunscreen, specifically designed for this project, will float above the roof and allow controlled natural light to filter into the galleries, eliminating the need for artificial illumination much of the time.

The three central pavilions on the main floor will serve as galleries for the display of smaller and environmentally-sensitive sculptures, as well as related paintings, prints, and drawings from the Nasher Collection. The two outer pavilions will house a café and store, while the lower level will include a smaller gallery for the display of light-sensitive works, a conservation lab, educational and research facilities, and an auditorium that opens to an outdoor terraced garden.

In addition to more than 10,000 square feet of indoor gallery space, the one and a half-acre sculpture garden will feature settings that frame the outdoor works. More than 170 trees, including cedar elms, live oaks, and magnolias, together with stone pathways, pools, and fountains, will define intimate landscapes for quiet reflection and contemplation of works, and create a verdant oasis in downtown Dallas. Approximately 25 large-scale sculptures from the Nasher Collection will be on view in the garden at any one time. *Tending, (Blue)* by James Turrell, is the only site-specific work commissioned as part of the sculpture garden. Turrell's free-standing "skyspace" will be situated at the north end of the garden, partially recessed in a landscaped berm.

The Collection

Developed over more than five decades, Raymond Nasher and his late wife Patsy began collecting art in 1950 and together formed one of the finest collections of 20th-century sculpture in the world. The Raymond and Patsy Nasher Collection includes masterpieces by Calder, de Kooning, di Suvero, Giacometti, Hepworth, Kelly, Matisse, Miró, Moore, Picasso, Rodin, and Serra, among many others, and continues to grow and evolve. One of the most recent acquisitions is a monumental cement sculpture by Pablo Picasso, *Head of a Woman* (1958).

The Nasher Collection has been presented in exhibitions at museums such as the National Gallery of Art, Washington, D.C.; the Centro de Arte Reina Sofia, Madrid, Spain; Forte di Belvedere, Florence, Italy; Tel Aviv Museum of Art, Tel Aviv, Israel; the California Palace of the Legion of Honor, San Francisco, California; the Solomon R. Guggenheim Museum, New York; and the Dallas Museum of Art.

The Dallas Arts District

The opening of the Nasher Sculpture Center represents a critical moment in the advancement of the Dallas Arts District and establishes a unique cultural and educational resource in Dallas that will attract visitors from around the world. The new institution will serve as a civic landmark, simultaneously advancing cultural tourism and enhancing the quality of life for local residents. Additional projects currently underway in the Arts District include the nearby Booker T. Washington High School for the Performing and Visual Arts, which is planning a renovation and expansion designed by architect Brad Cloepfil of Allied Works Architecture, and the Dallas Center for Performing Arts, which is developing a multiform theater designed by architect Rem Koolhaas of the Office for Metropolitan Architecture (OMA) and a 2,400-seat lyric theater designed by London-based Foster and Partners.

Raymond D. Nasher

Raymond D. Nasher was one of the first real estate developers to place art in his commercial complexes. His first retail shopping center in Dallas, NorthPark Center, was designed with the space necessary to display large-scale sculpture. Mr. Nasher has also played a leading role in the development and growth of all major arts organizations in Dallas. He established the Dallas Business Committee for the Arts in 1988 and has served as a board member of the Dallas Museum of Art, The Dallas Opera, The Dallas Symphony, the Dallas Theatre Center, Ballet Dallas, and the Modern Art Museum of Fort Worth. He has been appointed to the President's Committee on the Arts and Humanities by three presidents, and has also served on various committees and councils of numerous museums, including the Guggenheim in New York and the National Gallery in Washington, D.C.

Steven A. Nash

As the first Director of the Nasher Sculpture Center, Dr. Nash brings more than 30 years of directorial experience to this position. For 15 years, Dr. Nash served as Associate Director and Chief Curator at the Fine Arts Museums of San Francisco, where he was involved with development of the new M.H. de Young Memorial Museum plans, as well as with curatorial matters. Prior to that, from 1980-1988, he served in the roles of Deputy Director and Chief Curator at the Dallas Museum of Art. In his various museum posts, Dr. Nash has been instrumental in the acquisition of thousands of works of art, from all eras and cultures, and has organized many important exhibitions. He has also served on teams overseeing the construction of the new M.H. de Young Memorial Museum; an upgraded and expanded California Palace of the Legion of Honor; and the creation of a downtown facility for the Dallas Museum of Art.

Renzo Piano

Renzo Piano, winner of the 1998 Pritzker Prize for Architecture, has designed several critically acclaimed art museums, foremost among them the Beyeler Museum in Basel, the Menil Collection in Houston, and Georges Pompidou Centre in Paris (in collaboration with Richard Rogers). He has been praised as an architect who has the genius to meld art, architecture, and advanced engineering to create some of the most exciting museums in the world. In addition to his design for the Nasher Sculpture Center, Mr. Piano's current projects in the United States include: expansion of the Art Institute of Chicago; expansion of the High Museum of Art in Atlanta; new facilities for the Morgan Library in New York City; The California Academy of Sciences in San Francisco, CA; The New York Times building in New York City; and a master plan for Columbia University.

Peter Walker

Peter Walker, principal of Peter Walker and Partners of Berkeley, California, designed the landscapes at the Federal Triangle in Washington, D.C. (with I.M. Pei Architects); in Disney City in Orlando, Florida; at the Sony Center Berlin (with Murphy/Jahn Architects); and at the Toyota Municipal Museum of Art in Toyota City, Japan. He also designed the Tanner

Fountain at Harvard University in Cambridge, Massachusetts, and the Library Walk at the University of California at San Diego. Mr. Walker has also been teaching for more than 40 years and has served as chairman of the Landscape Architecture Department at the Harvard Graduate School of Design and at the University of California at Berkeley.

The Nasher Foundation

The development of the Nasher Sculpture Center, and costs for the acquisition of the land, landscaping, and construction of the facilities, is being fully funded by The Nasher Foundation. Under the direction of founding Chairman and President Raymond D. Nasher, The Nasher Foundation aims to care for and preserve the Nasher Collection, while enhancing its accessibility to the public. Other goals of The Foundation include: fostering scholarly research in the interpretation of modern and contemporary sculpture; supporting research studies on the conservation of sculpture; supporting art education programs; and developing other programs, principally in the arts, but also in public policy, medical research, and education.

For more information, please contact:

Jenifer Rogness
Richards/Gravelle
(phone number)
(e-mail address)

Krista Farber Weinstein
Nasher Sculpture Center
(phone number)
(e-mail address)

Becky Mayad
Richards/Gravelle
(phone number)
(e-mail address)

Reprinted with permission of Richards/Gravelle, Dallas, Texas.

(Sample op-ed)

Terri Schiavo's Lesson for Us All
By Patricia A. Bomba M.D., F.A.C.P.

What will happen if you experience a sudden illness that prevents you from making your own medical decisions? Will your family or loved ones know enough about what you value and believe to feel comfortable about making decisions about your care?

If there's a silver lining to the tragic case of Terri Schiavo, the 40-year-old Florida woman at the center of a legal battle between her husband and her family over her future care, it's that her situation has prompted these questions to be openly and thoughtfully discussed.

Everyone 18 years of age or older should express their health care preferences and end-of-life wishes to family members and their physician and put them in writing in a legal document called an *advance care directive*. This discussion and documentation process is known as *Advance Care Planning*, and it will spare your loved ones the emotional burden and turmoil that come with trying to guess what your wishes might have been, particularly during a medical crisis when you can't speak for yourself.

In 2002, *Means to a Better End*, the first national end-of-life report card, reported that just 15-20% of Americans have an advance care directive. That's probably because many people believe this is an issue solely for the elderly or the seriously ill.

The reality is that these conversations should begin when individuals are young, healthy and independent, and they should continue as our life experiences transform our views of what is important, and what we are willing to undergo in terms of medical treatments and interventions.

Advance Care Planning is a process that asks individuals to explore, clarify and put in writing their values, beliefs, goals of care and expectations. It requires them to name a legal spokesperson, and an alternate, who will work best with physicians and health care providers to make decisions on behalf of the patient. And it also requires them to complete the necessary legal documents, keep them up-to-date, and make them accessible to their spokesperson, provider, and others.

Here in New York State the process of advance care planning involves completing two documents; the Health Care Proxy and the New York Living Will.

The Health Care Proxy is a legal document that allows you to name someone to make decisions about your medical care if you can no longer speak for yourself. The New York Living Will allows you to state your wishes concerning your medical care in the event you develop an irreversible condition, if you become terminally ill, permanently unconscious or minimally conscious due to brain damage and will never regain the ability to make decisions.

If one begins to view Advance Care Planning as part of preventive health, then periodic review can be integrated with the concept of periodic health evaluation. By reviewing advance care directives along with nutrition, exercise, smoking, injury prevention, stress management, etc., the importance is clarified and the fear of discussion is demystified. Discussion can then be linked with the behavioral readiness to complete an advance care directive, which is Terri Schiavo's lesson for us all.

As a community service, Excellus BlueCross BlueShield offers a step-by-step booklet on Advance Care Planning. Copies can be obtained free of charge by calling the Excellus BlueCross BlueShield Customer Service Department, or by visiting the Health & Wellness section of the Excellus BlueCross BlueShield Web site at http://www.excellusbcbs.com.

Patricia Bomba, M.D., F.A.C.P., is Vice President and Medical Director/Geriatrics for Excellus BlueCross BlueShield and is a nationally recognized expert on Advance Care Planning.
Reprinted with permission of Excellus BlueCross BlueShield.

(Sample op-ed)

A Third Right Answer
By Elaine B. Agather

As I write this, the citizens of Dallas are facing two choices in the structure of our city government. And, frankly, neither one is very appealing. Choice 1—the status quo—has been a major concern to many of us for the past several years. Choice 2—the alternative proposed in the Blackwood petition—is far more drastic than necessary.

What's wrong with these choices? They do not address three components that must be present in a solution to reform our city government. First, the mayor must have clear authority over the executive functions of the city. Second, the respective responsibilities of the mayor and the council must be discernable so citizens can hold them accountable. Third, there must be sufficient and suitable checks and balances for our government to thrive with any office holder in any environment.

Choice 1—the status quo—clearly fails to provide a single point of authority over the executive functions, making accountability impossible. Neither the Mayor nor the City Council should continue to have the luxury of blaming poor performance on inadequacies of the system or lack of authority to perform duties.

Choice 2—the Blackwood amendment—fails to provide checks and balances. It does not merely enhance the powers of the mayor or eliminate the position of the city manager, but goes beyond to unnecessarily strip so many powers from the City Council that a proper legislative balance of the Mayor's near-absolute powers is almost nonexistent.

If neither of these choices will work, what would? What would fix the problem?

The Dallas Citizens Council has made several recommendations, and the City Council is incorporating those changes into a reasonable alternative that will be voted on by the Council on April 13. This third alternative is forward thinking, and it addresses all the shortfalls of the status quo and Blackwood.

The critical elements of City Council's alternative include empowering the mayor to hire the chief operating officer (no longer city manager) with the concurrence of the Council, and giving the mayor the authority to remove him or her at will. The mayor would also have authority and responsibility to concur in the hiring of the chiefs of the Police and Fire Departments.

Further, the mayor would work jointly with the chief operating officer to develop the budget for the city council's consideration. In addition, the office of the auditor would provide a voice to City Council in fiscal matters to enable a true check and balance in the legislative branch over finances.

The Council's alternative incorporates straightforward and easy-to-understand changes that accomplish the three necessary objectives for reform and that set our city on the right course for a strong future.

For those who find the status quo unacceptable and want a stronger mayor, they should applaud this council action.

For those opposed to Blackwood, this should be a welcome alternative. It has the best prospects of preventing an unacceptable charter revision from occurring.

City Council is on the right track. We urge the members to affirm their commitment to a stronger, better Dallas by voting at their next meeting to place this alternative on the ballot in November. This is a critical time for our city. We should all support our representatives' initiative and leadership and hold them accountable for giving voters a reasonable choice for change as soon as possible.

Elaine B. Agather is currently Chairman of the Dallas Citizens Council.
Reprinted with permission of Richards/Gravelle, Dallas, Texas.

(Sample fact sheet)

Fact Sheet

Project Description

The Nasher Sculpture Center is the first institution in the world dedicated exclusively to the exhibition of modern and contemporary sculpture with a collection of global significance as its foundation. Conceived by collector and philanthropist Raymond D. Nasher in consultation with museum professionals and scholars, the institution is distinguished by a groundbreaking facility and landscaped garden specifically designed for the indoor and outdoor display of sculpture.

The Raymond and Patsy Nasher Collection

Comprised of more than 300 sculptures, the Nasher Collection is one of the finest collections of modern sculpture in private or public hands, and includes masterpieces by Calder, de Kooning, di Suvero, Giacometti, Hepworth, Kelly, Matisse, Miró, Moore, Picasso, Rodin, and Serra, among many others.

Groundbreaking

January 2001

Opening

October 20, 2003 (Public opening)

Location

2001 Flora Street, Dallas, Texas Located in the heart of the downtown Dallas Arts District, the Nasher Sculpture Center occupies a site adjacent to the Dallas Museum of Art and the Morton H. Meyerson Symphony Center. The site is bounded by Harwood, Flora, and Olive Streets and the Woodall Rodgers Freeway.

Site

2.4 acres

Project Cost

$70 million (including land acquisition, landscaping, and construction costs)

Design Architect	Renzo Piano Building Workshop (Genoa, Italy)
Building Size	55,000 square feet
Total Indoor Gallery Space	10,000 square feet
Total Outdoor Exhibition Space	62,000 square feet
Design Features	The building is defined by parallel stone walls that form five equal-sized pavilions, each 112 feet long and 32 feet wide. The side walls are faced in two-inch wide slabs of Italian travertine, allowing for the facility's environmental and security systems to be concealed within. Each pavilion is enclosed by glass facades that allow the galleries to visually extend into the garden, providing unobstructed, continuous views from the street, through the building, and across the length of the garden.

A unique barrel-vaulted glass ceiling is suspended atop narrow steel ribs and supported by thin, stainless steel rods. Conceptually, the glass roof is a thin membrane that allows for the percolation of natural light into the galleries. The curved glass panels and building facades have a special low-iron composition producing the most transparent effect possible. Together, the glass ceiling and pavilion facades endow the architecture with a transparency and lightness.

An innovative sunscreen device, specifically designed for the project out of cast aluminum, will float above the roof and allow controlled natural light to filter into the galleries, eliminating the need for artificial illumination much of the time. The sun-shading mechanism was developed and engineered as an efficient means to admit the highest levels of ambient northern light into the galleries while simultaneously blocking out all direct sunlight. Unlike traditional galleries, this project required a higher level of natural illumination to activate the varied forms and surface textures of the sculpture.

Building Materials   Travertine, glass, steel, and oak

Building Facilities   *Ground Level:*

- Three central pavilions for the display of smaller and environmentally-sensitive sculptures, as well as related works in other media from the Raymond and Patsy Nasher Collection
- Café
- Nasher Store
- Boardroom

Lower Level:

- Gallery for the display of light-sensitive works
- Conservation lab
- Educational and research facilities, including library
- Auditorium
- Administrative offices

Landscape Architect   Peter Walker & Partners (Berkeley, California)

Garden Size	1.42 acres
Garden Features	• More than 170 oaks, elms, willows, pines, crape myrtles, and magnolias • 3 pools and fountains • Night lighting • Outdoor terraced garden • James Turrell site-specific "skyspace" installation
Founder	Mr. Raymond D. Nasher
Director	Dr. Steven A. Nash
Financing	The Nasher Foundation (a private foundation funded entirely by Mr. Nasher)
Hours & Admission	Tuesday–Sunday 11 AM to 6 PM; Thursday, 11 AM–9 PM $10 adults, $7 seniors, $5 students. Free for members and children under 12. The price of admission includes an audio tour.
Contact	Krista Farber Weinstein Nasher Sculpture Center (phone number) (e-mail address) Jenifer Rogness Richards/Gravelle (phone number) (e-mail address) Jacquelyn Burke/Ilana Simon Resnicow Schroeder Associates (phone number) (e-mail address)

Reprinted with permission of Richards/Gravelle, Dallas, Texas.

(Sample bio)

ARCHITECTURE TEAM

Renzo Piano, Architect

Renzo Piano, winner of the Pritzker Prize for Architecture in 1998, has designed several critically acclaimed art museums; foremost among them are the Beyeler Museum in Basel, the Menil Collection in Houston, and Georges Pompidou Centre in Paris (in collaboration with Richard Rogers). He has been praised as an architect who has the genius to meld art, architecture, and advanced engineering to create some of the most remarkable museums in the world. In addition to his work on art museums, Mr. Piano is noted for his design of the Kansai International Air Terminal in Osaka, Japan; the Museum of Science and Technology in Amsterdam; and a cultural center in Nouméa, New Caledonia. He was also involved in the monumental redevelopment of Berlin's Potsdamer Platz, both as master planner for the set of 15 buildings and as architect of 8 of them. Mr. Piano has also worked on the rehabilitation of historic buildings, including the Lingotto Factory renovation in Turin, Italy and the revitalization of the Old Harbor in Genoa, Italy, among many others. In addition to his design for the Nasher Sculpture Center, Mr. Piano's current projects include expansion of the Art Institute of Chicago; expansion of the High Museum of Art in Atlanta; new facilities for the Morgan Library in New York City; The California Academy of Sciences in San Francisco, CA; The New York Times building in New York City; and a master plan for Columbia University.

Peter Walker, Landscape Architect

Peter Walker has exerted a significant impact on the field of landscape architecture over a four-decade career. The scope of Mr. Walker's landscape projects is expansive and varied. It ranges from small gardens to new cities, corporate headquarters and academic campuses to urban plazas. Whether in urban or rural environments, his designs shape the landscape in a variety of stylistic and cultural inflections, always putting clarity and modernity of vision in the service of specific site requirements. Mr. Walker designed the landscapes at the Federal Triangle in Washington, D.C. (with I.M. Pei Architects); in Disney City in Orlando,

Florida; at the Sony Center Berlin (with Murphy/Jahn Architects); and at the Toyota Municipal Museum of Art in Toyota City, Japan. He also designed the Tanner Fountain at Harvard University in Cambridge, Massachusetts, and the Library Walk at the University of California at San Diego. Mr. Walker has also taught for more than 40 years and has served as chairman of the Landscape Architecture Department at the Harvard Graduate School of Design and at the University of California at Berkeley.

Reprinted with permission of Richards/Gravelle, Dallas, Texas.

(Sample pitch letter)

Dear (name):

We have a great health care story for you—the Framingham Heart Study will turn 50 in September. I know anniversary stories can be deadly, but I think that the birthday provides a good hook to look at what's new with what is arguably the most important epidemiological study in American history.

As an article published in the April issue of *JAMA* noted, "In 1948, postwar America was prospering. The nation's economic and military reputation had grown to new proportions. Unfortunately, so too had millions of Americans' risks for cardiovascular disease. Cigarette smoking was the norm and the typical diet didn't exactly skimp on the porterhouse."

Heart disease, similar to an infectious disease, had reached epidemic proportions and researchers wanted to know why. Over 5,000 healthy individuals between the ages of 30 and 60 (both men and women) were recruited from Framingham to help solve a major medical mystery. Why were so many people dying from heart attacks and other cardiovascular episodes? What were the causes and could the epidemic be stopped or at least mitigated?

"At the time," a member of the original Framingham Heart Study cohort now in his 80s said, "We had no idea what we were getting into, how this thing would grow and how much researchers would learn about preventing heart disease and its causes."

Before Framingham, who knew?—about cholesterol (either the "good or bad" kind), hypertension, smoking, and so many other risk factors associated with cardiovascular disease.

Before Framingham, who knew?—anything much about the unique manifestations of heart disease in women.

And, before Framingham, who knew?—that consuming endless big Macs and not eating your "veggies" could lead to a heart attack, by-pass or worse.

Renowned for its contributions advancing our understanding of the risk factors for heart disease and how to prevent it, Framingham Heart Study researchers continue this work, but also have expanded their horizons.

Utilizing the riches contained in the genetic data collected from two generations of Framingham families, today study researchers are searching for the molecular basis of disease and looking for new risk factors that may play a role in the development of cardiovascular disease. They also are investigating the causes of other serious disorders including osteoporosis and Alzheimer's.

If you are interested in pursuing a story, we can arrange interviews with members of intergenerational study participants, key researchers and the current and three former directors of the study. If you require a site visit, we can help with those arrangements as well.

Sincerely yours,

Barry Wanger
(phone number)

P.S. You'll find enclosed a press kit with background materials including information about the study's contributions to American medicine and current research projects.

Reprinted with permission of Wanger Associates, Newton, Mass.

(Sample e-mailed pitch letter)

When you were a child, did you go to bed naked? Or wear your street clothes as pajamas?

For many underprivileged youngsters, that is a way of life. Genevieve Piturro, the executive director and founder of the Pajama Program, is working to change that. She established the Manhattan-based charity to provide new pajamas to needy and abused children throughout the city and the nation. Operating on a shoestring budget and with a cadre of dedicated volunteers, the Program has given away more than 15,000 pjs. Kids in foster care facilities, homeless shelters, and group homes now go to bed feeling a little more loved and cared for in their brand new pajamas.

I would love to speak with you about a possible profile on the Pajama Program. I'm sure your viewers would want to hear about this unique charity. They may already have heard of it—the Program was lauded in the April 2005 issue of "O," Oprah Winfrey's magazine, as a unique concept. In the meantime, please visit www.pajamaprogram.org to learn more about the charity.

Thank you for your consideration.

Reprinted with permission of Jennefer Witter, president, The Boreland Group, Inc.

(Sample tip sheet)

How to handle report cards—the good, the bad and the ugly

MUNCIE, Ind.—Should you pay your child $10 for every "A"? Banish video games for a month for each "F"?

Lisa Huffman, assistant professor of educational psychology at Ball State University, offers these tips for handling report cards:

1. Keep lines of communication open. Ask your child how he feels about the school term before discussing the report card. For example, is she worried about what her marks may be? Be sure to let children know that discussing concerns is good. This way they will be more likely to let you know if there are any problems.

2. Take report cards seriously. While report cards don't tell the whole story, they do reflect how a student is progressing. Pay special attention to any grades that come as a surprise (good or bad). Encourage children to talk about school performance, again good or bad.

3. Praise a good report card. Be sure to let your child know that you are proud of his good work and accomplishments. This is a good time to post your child's work in a prominent place, such as a refrigerator. While celebrating successes also praise improvements in performance and commitments to working hard.

4. Talk about a bad report card. Failure can be scary, but if your child does not do as well as expected talk openly about it. Reassure your child that poor grades do not mean he is a failure. Poor report cards can be a catalyst for change and do not need to be a reason for punishment. You can work to develop a plan of action with goals for improvement.

5. Set realistic goals. It is probably not realistic to go from a "C" to an "A" on the next report card. However, a "B" seems realistic. Maybe completing all homework on time or achieving an "A" on two or more assignments in a particular topic is your goal. Encourage your child to do her best.

6. Don't assume an "A" reflects your child's best efforts. Talk to her about the ease with which she completes course work—maybe it is not challenging enough.

7. Look at your child's work regularly. Report cards only come out a few times a year. Review your student's work regularly and pay special attention to grades and comments that go along with them. This will help you and your student identify trouble spots before it is too late.

8. Encourage good work habits and effort. Poor grades on report cards may not reflect inability, but rather insufficient effort. When your child is studying or doing homework this is a good time for you also to do something quietly, which will lessen distractions.

9. Be involved in your child's school. Children who do well in school have parents who are actively involved in their children's education and their school. Volunteer at school or help your child with her homework.

10. Incentives can be rewarding when children do well or meet goals. However, they should not be bribes. Rather than telling children you will give them money for good grades before they have even earned them, surprise them after the grades are earned with a small gift or some special time. Be sure to praise effort and improvement along with good grades. Children should want good grades out of interest, pride, and an understanding that success in school is necessary for success in life. Children should not earn good grades only because they will get a reward.

Ball State University, located in Muncie, Ind., is the third-largest public university in Indiana, with more than 18,000 students. Originally a private teacher training school when it opened in 1899, Ball State became a university in 1965. Ball State, with its 1,035-acre campus, has many nationally ranked programs and highly touted immersion-learning experiences.

For more information, contact Huffman at (phone number) or (e-mail address)

– 30 –

Layne Cameron
3/22/05

Reprinted with permission of Layne Cameron, media relations manager, Ball State University.

(Sample tip sheet)

Contact: Norman Birnbach (phone number) (e-mail address)

Handling the December Holidays:
Eight Tips from InterfaithFamily.com

Okay, so you are intermarried, and have to deal with both Christmas and Hanukkah. What to do? According to experts who have written for InterfaithFamily.com, a free Internet magazine for intermarried families, here are some tips:

1. If you are raising Jewish children and don't know what to do about Christmas (or if you are raising Christian children and don't know what to do about Hanukkah), our experts say that it is okay to participate in the holiday as a way of respecting the non-Jewish (or Jewish) spouse and family. You can tell your kids, "Today we're going to Grandma's house for Christmas because that is Daddy's (or Mommy's) holiday. We'll help him and his family celebrate, just as he helps us celebrate Hanukkah."

2. Keep the focus on the children's needs. What kids most love about Christmas is not the presents but the family togetherness. You don't need to focus on the gifts; it is having the family all together which will make it most meaningful for your children. And help children understand that they can enjoy Christmas and Hanukkah activities without betraying either parent or their religious upbringing. At the same time, use holidays to reinforce children's religious identity.

3. If you are raising Jewish kids and they feel uncomfortable about singing Christmas carols in school, should you complain to the school or reassure your kids? Our experts say you can do both. You might speak with the principal of the school about broadening the holiday song repertoire to include singing Hanukkah songs. That way, your child would be singing both Christmas and Hanukkah songs, as would the other kids. You can also reassure your children that singing the Christmas holiday songs doesn't make them Christian, nor does enjoying those songs. It is okay to enjoy other people's holidays, as long as your kids are clear what *their* holidays are.

4. Should you tell your in-laws that they shouldn't give your children Christmas stockings or presents (if you are raising them Jewish) or Hanukkah presents (if you are raising them Christian)? That is up to you. Some parents ask the grandparents to give gifts wrapped in paper that indicates the holiday the children *do* celebrate, and that includes all the relevant paraphernalia. There is no right answer for everyone. Do what works for you and your family.

5. If your children want a Christmas tree in your home and your Jewish spouse refuses, how should you handle it? Perhaps you had an agreement to celebrate Christmas at the grandparents' home, but now your kids (and you) want to celebrate in the home. Situations do change over time. Perhaps it is time for you and your partner to sit down for a talk. It would be important for each of you to explain what the holiday means to you. Share memories of when you were a child, how your grandparents celebrated with you, and what about those memories and traditions make them meaningful for you. Be clear about what the underlying issues are. Is it your own reluctance to have a Christmas tree or menorah in your home, or your fear about how your relatives might react?

6. Remember, the main concern is to decide how your family will live religiously throughout the year, not just for the month of December. If you agree about how you will live the rest of the year, then giving in on this holiday is less significant.

7. Allow your initial decisions to change as you and your family evolve. Certain things that may have seemed important at one stage of your marriage may become less important later. But pay attention to your *inner* feelings, to whether or not you feel comfortable with the practices your family evolves.

8. Work as partners to develop new family traditions while recognizing each partner's needs and work out ways to meet them. Denying a need will breed resentment, whereas negotiating a mutually acceptable way to meet it will validate what is most important to your partner, strengthening your relationship. Creating ways to celebrate aspects of the holidays in your home, in your own style, unites the family.

Reprinted with permission of Birnbach Communications.

(Sample PSA scripts—each script illustrates how the same concept is executed in different time lengths)

Prescription for Poverty :30

For the billions who suffer from poverty, there is a cure.

A cure that doesn't just treat the symptoms, but stops poverty before it spreads.

CARE is proven effective in fighting poverty. Combining experience, innovation and other powerful ingredients, CARE brings permanent relief to one community after another.

No harmful side effects. Only a better, more stable world for all.

CARE. Where the end of poverty begins.

A Plague :10

There's a plague infecting half the world.

It's poverty.

And the cure is in your hands.

CARE.

Reprinted with permission of Goodwill Communications, Inc.

A Cure for Poverty :60

Like a plague, poverty infects half the world's people.

It's a ruthless killer, striking down men and women in the prime of life, claiming children who are defenseless against its wrath.

But there is a cure for poverty. And it's in your hands.

Through CARE, you can help people in the world's poorest communities fight for their lives—and make a complete and permanent recovery.

CARE overcomes poverty through agriculture, education, health care, small business and more. Remedies that work together, helping poor people target the source of the problem, not just the symptoms.

And that's a cure that can last a lifetime.

To learn more, call 1 800 521-CARE, or log onto care.org.

CARE. Where the end of poverty begins.

A Cure for Poverty :30

Like a plague, poverty infects half the world's people.

It's a ruthless killer, striking innocent children and their families.

But there is a cure. And it's in your hands.

Through CARE, you can help communities permanently recover from poverty.

Because CARE targets the source of the problem, not just the symptoms.

That's a cure that can last a lifetime.

CARE. Where the end of poverty begins.

A Cure for Poverty :10

There's a plague infecting half the world.

It's poverty.

And the cure is in your hands.

CARE.

Message Development Worksheet

Message Point 1

Headline: _____

_____

Supporting anecdote, information, statistic, etc. _____

_____

_____

_____

Message Point 2

Headline: _____

_____

Supporting anecdote, information, statistic, etc. _____

_____

_____

_____

Message Point 3

Headline: _____

_____

Supporting anecdote, information, statistic, etc. _____

_____

_____

_____

News Release Writing Worksheet

FOR IMMEDIATE RELEASE (or Release Date)

Most releases can be used immediately. If that's the case, write FOR IMMEDIATE RELEASE. If the information can't be used before a specific date or time, it's FOR RELEASE (INSERT DATE AND TIME).

What's your situation?

_____

Contact name, phone number, and e-mail address

Who should get calls from reporters?

_____

_____

Attention-getting headline

Announce the release subject with active verbs and colorful words.

_____

_____

Lead paragraph

Summarize your news in one sentence. Add a second sentence with a few more details. Read them over—do they say what they should? Make sure the sentences aren't too long.

_____

_____

Five *Ws* and One *H*

Who, what, when, where, why, and how? You might have answered some of these questions in the lead paragraph. Answer the rest in the next two or three paragraphs.

_____

_____

Quote

Does this release warrant a quote? Who is being quoted? What is the gist of that person's comments?

_____

_____

Paragraph about your company

Conclude your release with a boilerplate paragraph that summarizes what your organization does.

_____

_____

Tip Sheet Writing Worksheet

FOR IMMEDIATE RELEASE (or Release Date)

Most tip sheets can be used immediately. If that's the case, write FOR IMMEDIATE RELEASE. If the information can't be used before a specific date or time, it's FOR RELEASE (INSERT DATE AND TIME). What's your situation?

Contact name, phone number, and e-mail address.

Who should get calls from reporters?

Attention-getting headline

Include the number of tips—"Five Ways to . . ." or "Ten Tips for . . . ." Use active, colorful words.

Lead paragraph

What's the situation? Why is this advice necessary?

The expert

Who is the expert (name, title, any other necessary credentials)?

Quote

What does the expert offering the tips have to say about the subject?

The tips

Use bullets or numbers when listing the tips in punchy, pithy, how-to language.

1. Tip
2. Tip
3. Tip
4. Tip
5. Tip
6. Tip
7. Tip
8. Tip
9. Tip
10. Tip

Paragraph about your company

Conclude your tip sheet with a boilerplate paragraph that summarizes what your organization does.

Press Conference Checklist

Beforehand . . .
Event planning
_____ Select appropriate date, time, place
_____ Reserve best location for event size, personality, and budget
_____ Select speakers
_____ Develop invitation lists—media and others
_____ Create and mail invitations
_____ Arrange for food and beverages
_____ Write script
_____ Hire photographer
_____ Assign on-site responsibilities to staff
_____ Rehearse speakers
_____ Make follow-up calls to invitees who have not responded
_____ Send reminder media alert to press
_____ Create event timetable
_____ Create staff list that outlines responsibilities
_____ Arrange for on-site AV equipment, telephones, and specific technical capabilities if needed
_____ Discuss room set-up with facility
_____ Create press materials
_____ Create checklist of RSVP'd guests for use on-site

Invitations—include:
_____ Date and start time with brief agenda
_____ Street location of venue and parking information if necessary
_____ Brief description of press conference purpose
_____ Names and titles of speakers
_____ RSVP name, phone number/e-mail, and deadline
_____ Indication of food and beverages offered (coffee and snacks, cocktails, breakfast buffet, etc.)

On-Site
Room set-up
_____ Electrical outlets—are they where you need them to be?
_____ Light switches for room darkening if required for presentation
_____ AV equipment: Is it what you need? Does it work?
_____ Telephones
_____ Food and beverage set-up
_____ Registration desk
_____ Nametags (if used)
_____ Signage
_____ Chairs
_____ Coat check
_____ Name cards for speakers (if on a panel)
_____ Display materials, including products
_____ Raised platform for speakers
_____ Press materials
_____ RSVP checklist at registration table
_____ Pens and pads of paper at registration table

Speaker set-up
_____ Table
_____ Chairs
_____ Podium
_____ Props
_____ Name cards for speakers (if on a panel)
_____ Script
_____ Microphone
_____ AV materials (PowerPoint presentation? Flip chart? Poster board?)

Publicity Plan Worksheet

Situation/Overview

_____

_____

Audiences

-
-
-

Goals

-
-
-

Strategy

_____

_____

Tactics

-
-
-

Objectives

-
-
-

Budget
(Itemize estimated expenses; include staff time if appropriate.)

Timeline

Week/Month for Activity	Activity

Public Relations Agency Evaluation Grid

Agency: _____

Quality or characteristic	How important is this quality to your company or the project, on a scale of 1 to 5? (1 is the lowest, 5 is the highest)	How do you rank the agency for this quality on a scale of 1 to 5? (1 is the lowest, 5 is the highest)
Agency size		
Overall publicity and public relations capability		
Media relations experience		
Writing skills		
In-person communication skills		
Knowledge of your field		
Experience working with nonprofit organizations		
Whether the agency was referred to you by more than one source		
Your impression of its ability to meet deadlines		
Creativity		
Chemistry with your group		
Reputation		
TOTAL OF ALL ROWS